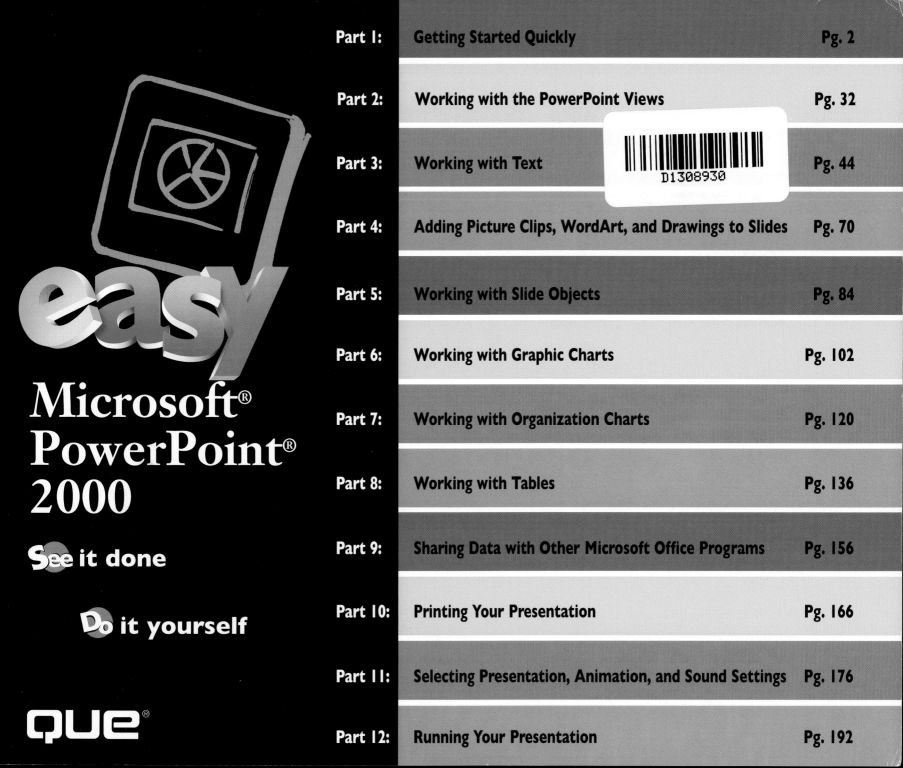

easy
Microsoft® PowerPoint® 2000

See it done

Do it yourself

que®

D1308930

Copyright© 1999 by Que® Corporation

All rights reserved. Printed in the United States of America. No part of this book may be used or reproduced in any form or by any means, or stored in a database or retrieval system, without prior written permission of the publisher except in the case of brief quotations embodied in critical articles and reviews. Making copies of any part of this book for any purpose other than your own personal use is a violation of United States copyright laws. For information, address Que Corporation, 201 W. 103rd Street, Indianapolis, IN 46290. You may reach Que's direct sales line by calling 1-800-428-5331.

Library of Congress Catalog No.: 98-86861

ISBN: 0-7897-1846-4

This book is sold as is, without warranty of any kind, either express or implied, respecting the contents of this book, including but not limited to implied warranties for the book's quality, performance, merchantability, or fitness for any particular purpose. Neither Que Corporation nor its dealers or distributors shall be liable to the purchaser or any other person or entity with respect to any liability, loss, or damage caused or alleged to have been caused directly or indirectly by this book.

02 01 00 99   6 5 4 3 2 1

Interpretation of the printing code: the rightmost double-digit number is the year of the book's printing; the rightmost single-digit number, the number of the book's printing. For example, a printing code of 99-1 shows that the first printing of the book occurred in 1999.

Trademarks

All terms mentioned in this book that are known to be trademarks or service marks have been appropriately capitalized. Que cannot attest to the accuracy of this information. Use of a term in this book should not be regarded as affecting the validity of any trademark or service mark.

Screen reproductions in this book were created using Collage Plus from Inner Media, Inc., Hollis, NH.

About the Author

Laura Stewart is a professional instructor with more than seven years experience teaching computer application classes. She is the author of *Easy Microsoft PowerPoint 97* and *Easy Microsoft Excel 97*. Laura has also been a contributing author on several other Que computer reference books, including *Special Edition Using Microsoft PowerPoint 97*.

ECCE QUAM BONUM

Acknowledgements

Publishing a book like this has been a unique and enjoyable challenge for me. Several people have been key in ensuring this is the most complete and comprehensive visual learning PowerPoint 2000 book possible, and they deserve my thanks. Jill Byus and Jim Grey led the team of Que professionals who defined and edited this book. Their assistance in its production, with particular focus on creating realistic presentation examples, greatly improved the book you now hold.

Several other important people have been instrumental in developing this book, especially Karen Walsh, Susan Daffron, and Barbara Hacha. They did a superb job of editing the grammatical, logical, and technical content of this book, making several significant suggestions that have greatly improved this Easy PowerPoint book. Thanks also to John Rahm for his proofreading expertise and Lisa England for making the pages look good.

Dedication

This book is dedicated to Edmund Stewart, Jr., the best brother a girl could ever have. Okay, so he's my only brother…he's still the best.

Executive Editor
Jim Minatel

Acquisitions Editor
Jill Byus

Development Editor
Jim Grey

Technical Editor
Susan Daffron

Managing Editor
Thomas F. Hayes

Project Editor
Karen A. Walsh

Copy Editor
Barbara Hacha

Indexer
Chris Barrick

Book Designer
Jean Bisesi

Cover Designer
Anne Jones

Proofreader
John Rahm

Layout
Lisa England

Illustrations
Bruce Dean

How to Use This Book

It's as Easy as 1-2-3

Each part of this book is made up of a series of short, instructional lessons, designed to help you understand basic information that you need to get the most out of your computer hardware and software.

Click: Click the left mouse button once.

Double-click: Click the left mouse button twice in rapid succession.

Right-click: Click the right mouse button once.

Pointer Arrow: Highlights an item on the screen you need to point to or focus on in the step or task.

Selection: Highlights the area onscreen discussed in the step or task.

Click & Type: Click once where indicated and begin typing to enter your text or data.

 Tips and Warnings give you a heads-up for any extra information you may need while working through the task.

2 Each task includes a series of quick, easy steps designed to guide you through the procedure.

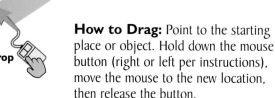

Drag

Drop

How to Drag: Point to the starting place or object. Hold down the mouse button (right or left per instructions), move the mouse to the new location, then release the button.

1 Each step is fully illustrated to show you how it looks onscreen.

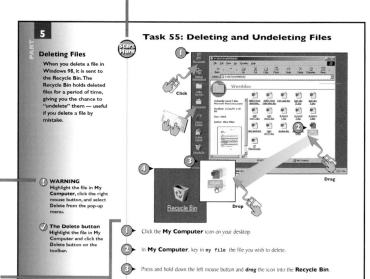

Task 55: Deleting and Undeleting Files

Page 96

3 Items that you select or click in menus, dialog boxes, tabs, and windows are shown in **bold**. Information you type is in a `special font`. Glossary terms are shown in ***bold italic***.

Next Step: If you see this symbol, it means the task you're working on continues on the next page.

End Task: Task is complete.

Introduction

Someone once said, "If it's not easy, why bother?" That's exactly why Que created the Easy series of books. If you're like most computer users, you want to know the easiest way to learn new software. You don't have time to sit and read paragraphs and paragraphs of information in computer books the size of Webster's unabridged dictionary. You need to be able to produce great-looking presentations quickly and easily. Right? If this sounds familiar, then you're holding the right book.

Easy Microsoft PowerPoint 2000 approaches learning *visually*. It is a step-by-step illustrated guide to the most essential PowerPoint tasks. You can use PowerPoint to create formal presentations or briefings for clients, supervisors, and colleagues. You can create presentations that can easily be turned into Web pages for your company's intranet or added to an Internet Web site. You can also use PowerPoint to prepare bulletin board flyers or signs. Once created, a presentation can be displayed on an overhead projection system, shipped off to have 35mm slides created, printed on acetate, or printed as handouts for your audience.

This book is divided into 12 distinct color-coded parts. Within each part are a series of one- to two-page tasks. Each task contains a brief description of the task and a series of step-by-step screen examples to guide you through the task. By following the visual steps, you will learn how to accomplish the task.

One or two sentences at the bottom of each page describe each step. In the page margins are tips and warnings. Tips provide hints on performing a task and contain additional information about the steps you are learning or references to other related tasks. Warnings help you to avoid complications or pitfalls as you work with PowerPoint.

This book is designed for the person who is not familiar with PowerPoint, but who knows a little about Windows and how to use a mouse. With that background, this book shows you how to create and modify dynamic PowerPoint presentations quickly and easily. You can use this book as a tutorial for learning PowerPoint by reading it front to back, or you can use it as a reference guide to look up the steps for a specific task. In the back of the book, a detailed index will help you look up topics and features this book presents.

Tell Us What You Think

As the reader of this book, *you* are our most important critic and commentator. We value your opinion and want to know what we're doing right, what we could do better, what areas you'd like to see us publish in, and any other words of wisdom you're willing to pass our way.

As the Executive Editor for the General Desktop Applications team at Que, I welcome your comments. You can fax, email, or write me directly to let me know what you did or didn't like about this book—as well as what we can do to make our books stronger.

Please note that I cannot help you with technical problems related to the topic of this book, and that due to the high volume of mail I receive, I might not be able to reply to every message.

When you write, please be sure to include this book's title and author, as well as your name and phone or fax number. I will carefully review your comments and share them with the author and editors who worked on the book.

Fax: 317-581-4666

Email: office_que@mcp.com

Mail: Executive Editor
          General Desktop Applications
          Macmillan Computer Publishing
          201 West 103rd Street
          Indianapolis, IN 46290 USA

Getting Started Quickly

Welcome to PowerPoint 2000! PowerPoint is an exciting program you can use to create dynamic presentations, briefings, or flyers. With PowerPoint, you can print acetate slides, audience handouts, and notes pages.

This part of the book is designed to acquaint you with PowerPoint. You will learn to quickly create, save, and print a simple PowerPoint presentation. Additionally, you will learn about the various parts of the PowerPoint screen, how to move from slide to slide in your presentation, and how to use the built-in Help screens. This part also shows you how to add a professional design to the background of your slides and provides useful tips on creating effective presentations.

Tasks

Task 1: Starting Microsoft PowerPoint

Opening PowerPoint

You can start Microsoft PowerPoint by using the Start button on the Windows taskbar.

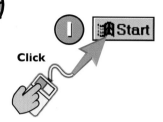

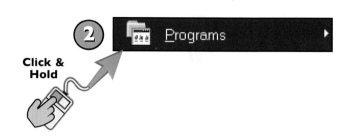

Click

Click & Hold

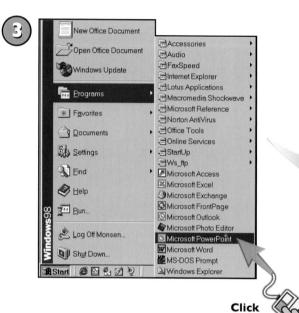

Click

✓ **The Office Assistant**
When you first open PowerPoint the Office Assistant, Clippit, may appear. Clippit, an animated paperclip figure, is there to help you as you work in PowerPoint.

1. Click the **Start** button on the Windows taskbar.

2. Position the mouse pointer on **Programs**.

3. Click **Microsoft PowerPoint**. The initial PowerPoint screen appears.

End Task

Task 2: Creating a Simple Presentation

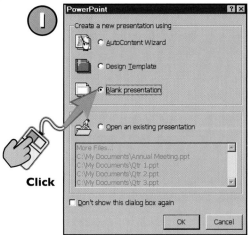

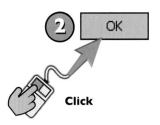

Click

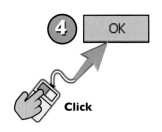

Click

Starting a New Presentation from the Initial PowerPoint Screen

You can either create a new presentation or open an existing presentation from the initial **PowerPoint** window.

✓ **Identifying Slide Layouts**
When you click a layout, a description appears in the lower-right corner of the dialog box.

✓ **Creating More Presentations**
See Part 1, Task 14 to learn how to create additional presentations while working in PowerPoint.

---

1. Click **Blank presentation** to create a new PowerPoint presentation.

2. Click **OK**. The New Slide dialog box appears.

3. Click an AutoLayout from the samples displayed. Scroll to see additional layout options.

4. Click **OK**. The slide appears with the layout you chose.

Understanding the Tri-pane View

By default, PowerPoint shows you the current slide and some related information in the **Normal** view, which has three panes.

Task 3: Introducing the PowerPoint Window

Start Here

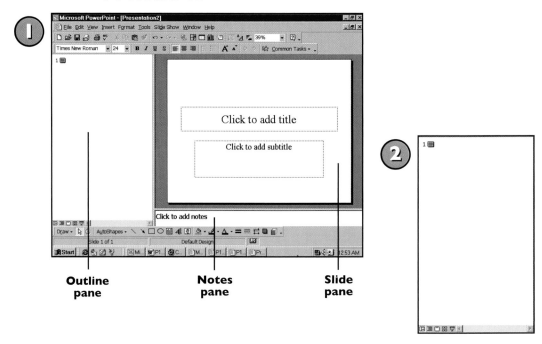

Outline pane

Notes pane

Slide pane

Click to add notes

✓ **Moving from Pane to Pane**

You can click a pane to activate it or press **F6** to cycle among the panes.

1 The Normal view comprises three panes: the Outline pane, the Slide pane, and the Notes pane.

2 The Outline pane shows the organization of your presentation's slides. You can create slides and rearrange paragraphs and slides in this pane.

3 The Notes pane lets you add and view your speaker notes, which are notes you can use to describe the slide details.

Next Step

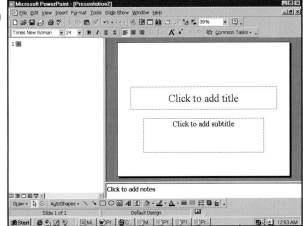

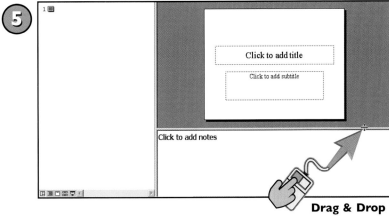

Drag & Drop

 Using the PowerPoint Views
See Part 2 to learn how to use each of the PowerPoint views.

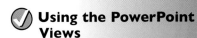 **Adding Text to Slides**
See Part 3 to learn how to add bulleted lists, numbered lists, and independent text to slides.

4 The Slide pane shows you how the active slide looks. You can add text, pictures, and sound clips in the Slide pane.

5 You can change the size of a pane by dragging the pane border. Look for the mouse pointer to become a set of parallel lines with arrows before you drag.

Getting Acquainted with PowerPoint

The PowerPoint window has features similar to those found in other Microsoft Office programs (such as Word or Excel)—for example, the menu bar, toolbars, and shortcut menus.

Task 4: Using the Window Elements

Start Here

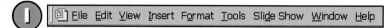

① File Edit View Insert Format Tools Slide Show Window Help

②

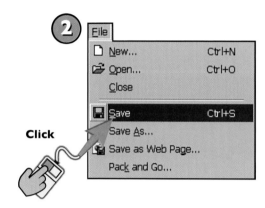

File	
New...	Ctrl+N
Open...	Ctrl+O
Close	
Save	Ctrl+S
Save As...	
Save as Web Page...	
Pack and Go...	

Click

③ File Edit View Insert Format Tools Slide Show Window Help

✓ **Inactive Options**

When menu choices and toolbar icons appear grayed-out, they are unavailable to you. See Part 1, Task 5, to customize the way menus and toolbars behave.

① The menu bar appears at the top of the PowerPoint window. It organizes the PowerPoint commands.

② Click a menu to see the list of its commands. Toolbar icons appear before, and keyboard shortcuts after, many commands.

③ By default, the Standard and Formatting toolbars share one line underneath the menu bar. A double vertical line indicates the beginning of a toolbar.

Next Step

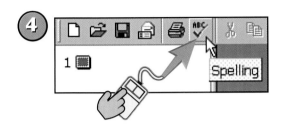

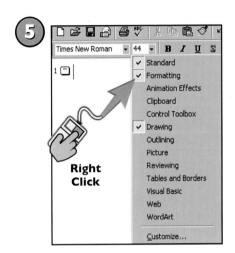

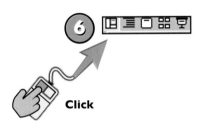

Click

④ Position the mouse pointer over a button until you see a **ScreenTip** that tells you which command the icon represents.

⑤ Right-click slide objects or parts of the screen to see shortcut menus.

⑥ Use the View buttons (located in the lower-left corner of the PowerPoint screen) to switch between the PowerPoint views—Normal, Outline, Slide, Slide Sorter, and Slide Show.

⑦ The status bar indicates the current slide number, the total number of slides, and the background design being used on the presentation.

✓ **Why Are Shortcut Menus Useful?**
Use shortcut menus to display a specific set of commands used with parts of the screen or with slide objects.

✓ **Displaying Other Slides**
See Part 1, Task 9 for specific steps on moving from slide to slide. See Part 1, Task 10 for information on changing the Presentation Design.

Task 5: Setting Menu and Toolbar Options

Showing All Menu Commands and Toolbar Icons

By default, the PowerPoint menus and toolbars show only the most popular commands. For someone just learning PowerPoint, it is useful to display all the menu commands and toolbar icons.

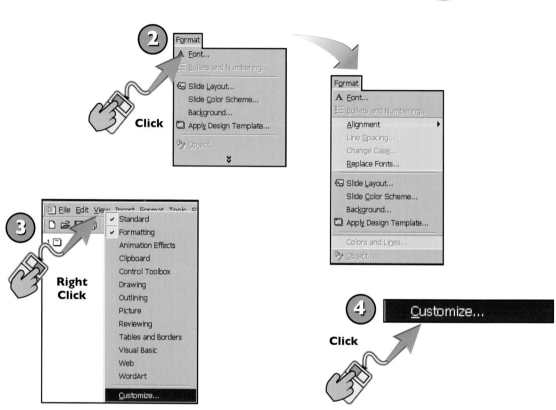

✓ **Personalized Menus**
If you choose not to display all menu commands, PowerPoint adapts to you. PowerPoint adds commands you frequently use to the default list of displayed commands.

① By default, the Standard and Formatting toolbars are displayed on one line. The beginning of a toolbar is marked by a set of double vertical lines.

② By default, a menu shows the most commonly used commands. If you pause over the menu, the entire set of commands appears.

③ To change the default display settings, right-click the **menu bar** or any toolbar.

④ Then click **Customize** on the shortcut menu.

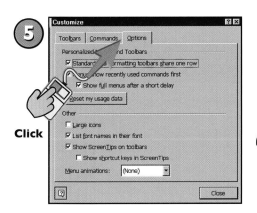

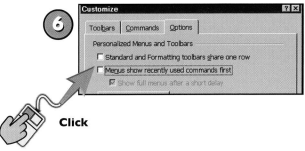

Click

Click

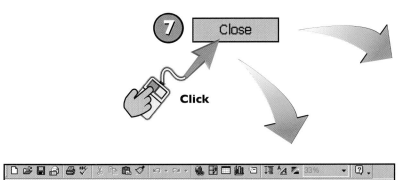

Click

✓ **Understanding Personalized Menus**
The expanded version of a menu (shown in Step 2) can be confusing. The dark gray background, or raised look, indicates commands that appeared when you first displayed the menu— the most recently used commands.

✓ **Customizable Toolbars**
The drop-down arrow at the end of each toolbar provides a quick way to add or remove icon buttons from toolbars.

5 In the Customize dialog box, click the **Options** tab.

6 Click to remove the check marks from the first two options: **Standard and Formatting toolbars share one row** and **Menus show recently used commands first**.

7 Click **Close**. The Formatting toolbar appears below the Standard toolbar and the menus show all commands.

Task 6: Working with "Click" Placeholders

Understanding Slide Placeholders

Most slide layouts contain placeholders you can use to add text, charts, and picture clips. These placeholders control the size and format of the objects.

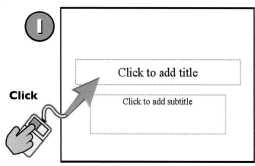

Click

Click to add title

Click to add subtitle

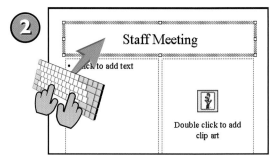

Staff Meeting

Click to add text

Double click to add clip art

Staff Meeting

- Agenda
  - Committee Reports
  - Old Issues
  - New Issues
  - Assignment of Tasks
  - Summary

Editing "Click" Placeholders

When you click a text placeholder, such as a title or bulleted list, a flashing cursor appears to indicate you are editing the placeholder.

1 Click anywhere inside a placeholder to activate it. This figure shows the Title Slide Layout, which contains two placeholders: one for the title and the other for a subtitle.

2 Begin typing the text you want. This figure shows a slide layout with three "click" placeholders.

3 This figure shows a slide that contains a completed title, a bulleted list, and a picture clip object. See Part 4 to learn how to add clips to your slides.

Task 7: Adding New Slides

Start Here

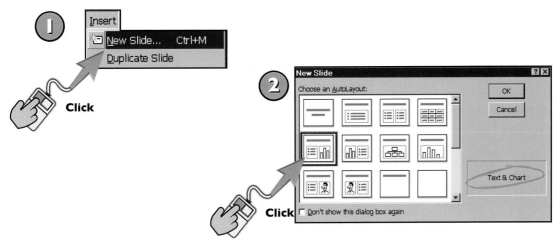

Click

Click

Click

Adding More Slides to Your Presentation

Each slide you create can have a different layout, or arrangement, of text and graphics.

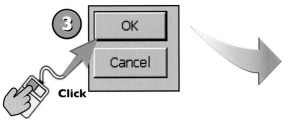

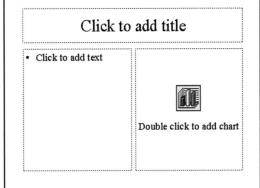

① Choose **Insert**, **New Slide**.

② Click a slide layout. A brief description of the layout appears in the lower-right corner of the dialog box.

③ Click **OK**. PowerPoint adds a slide to your presentation using the layout you selected.

✔ **Scroll to See Additional Slide Layouts**
Drag the scrollbar in the New Slide dialog box to see other slide layout choices.

✔ **Creating Graphic Charts**
See Part 6 to learn how to create graphic charts in PowerPoint.

Task 8: Changing the Slide Layout

Choosing a Different Slide Layout

You can easily change the arrangement and type of "click" placeholders on a slide by selecting a different slide layout.

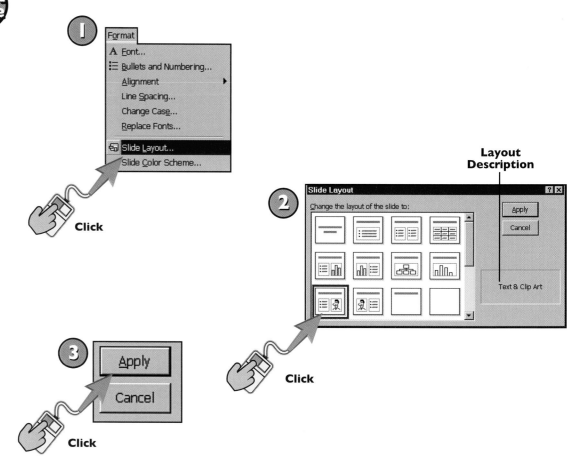

Layout Description

Text & Clip Art

Click

Click

Click

✓ **Common Tasks**
If the Formatting toolbar is displayed, use the **Common Tasks** button to change the slide layout.

✓ **Adding Clip Art Images to Slides**
See Part 4, Task I to learn how to add picture clips to your presentation.

1 Choose **Format**, **Slide Layout**.

2 Click the new layout to apply to the slide. Read the description for the selected layout in the lower-right corner to ensure you selected the correct layout.

3 Click **Apply** to change the slide layout.

Task 9: Moving from Slide to Slide

Start Here

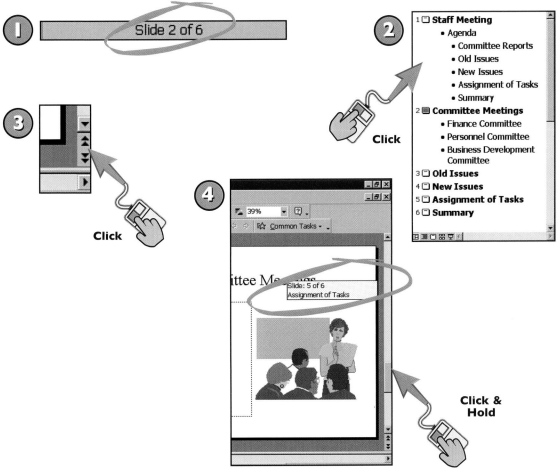

① Slide 2 of 6

③ Click

④

② Click

Click & Hold

Displaying Other Slides

Most presentations consist of several slides. You can move forward or backward in your presentation with a few mouse clicks.

① Look at the slide indicator on the status bar to determine which slide is active.

② If the slide you want to display appears in the Outline pane, click anywhere in the slide's text to make it the active slide.

③ To browse through one slide at a time, click the **Previous Slide** or the **Next Slide** button (in the lower-right corner of the PowerPoint window).

④ To move to a specific slide in the presentation, drag the scroll box until the yellow pop-up box displays the title and number of the slide you want.

 Dragging the Scroll Box
If you have not added titles to your slides, the yellow pop-up ScreenTip (Step 4) displays only the slide numbers as you drag the scroll box.

 End Task

Task 10: Applying a Presentation Design

Changing the Appearance of the Presentation

PowerPoint includes a set of presentation design templates that quickly gives your presentation a professional appearance.

Start Here

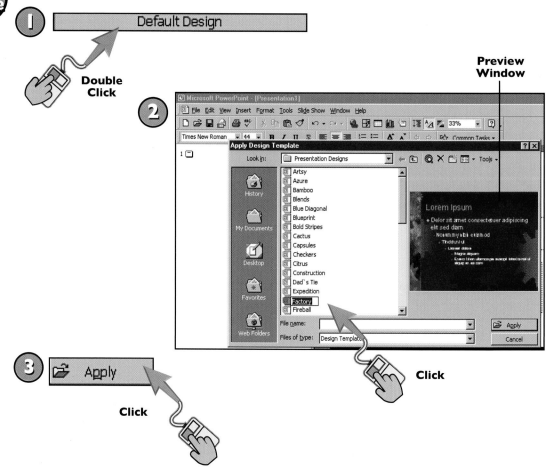

Preview Window

1 Default Design

Double Click

Click

3 Apply

Click

1 Double-click the design name indicator on the status bar. The Apply Design Template dialog box appears.

2 From the Presentations Designs Folder, click a design to apply to your presentation. A sample of the design appears to the right, in the preview window.

3 Click **Apply**.

Task 11: Saving Your Presentation

Click

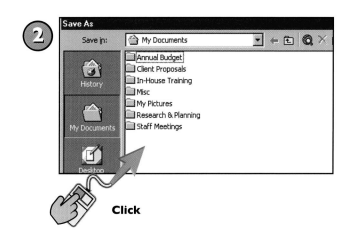

Click

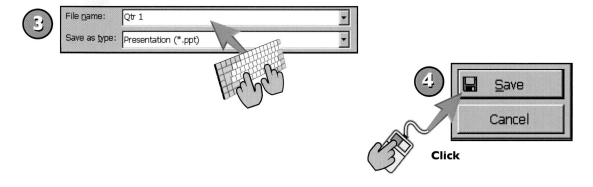

Click

Saving Your Work

Whether you have created a new file or are making changes to an existing presentation, be sure you save your presentations often.

✓ Saving a Copy of the Presentation
To save a copy of a file and keep the original unchanged, use the **File, Save As** command and give the copy a new name.

! WARNING
The following characters cannot be used in file-names:
/ \ > < * ? " | : ;

1. Click the **Save** button. (If you saved this file at least once before, this is all you have to do.)

2. From the **Save in** drop-down list, choose the folder in which you want to store the presentation.

3. Click in the **File name** box and type the name for the presentation. The name can be no longer than 255 characters.

4. Click **Save**.

End Task

Task 12: Printing Your Slides

Creating Printed Output

Before you print the presentation, use the **Slide Show** feature to preview your PowerPoint presentation. This will give you the opportunity to catch any errors, so that you don't waste paper printing mistakes. Then choose the print options you need.

(!) **WARNING**
If you click the **Print** button located on the Standard toolbar, your presentation is sent to the printer immediately—the Print dialog box does not display. If the default print setting is for color and your printer prints only black-and-white, your printed slides will look awful.

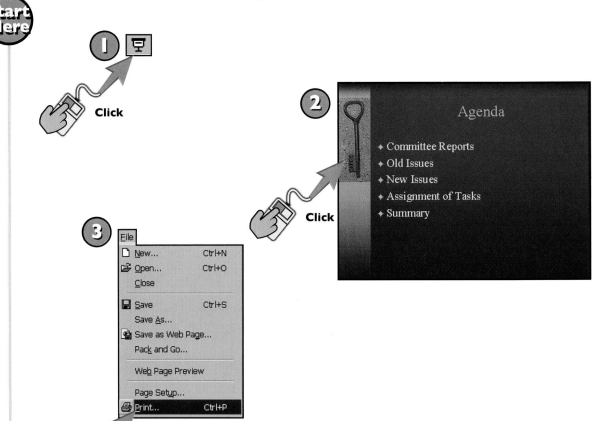

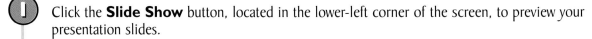

(1) Click the **Slide Show** button, located in the lower-left corner of the screen, to preview your presentation slides.

(2) Click the left mouse button each time you want to advance to the next slide in the presentation. On the last slide, clicking the mouse exits the Slide Show.

(3) Choose **File**, **Print** to display the Print dialog box.

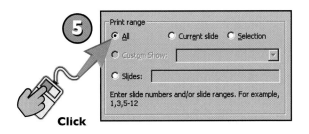

Click

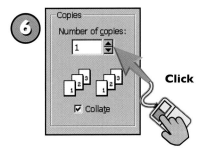

Click

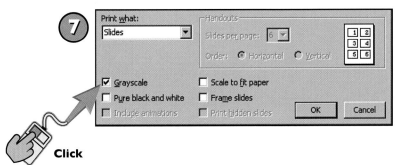

Click

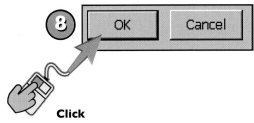

Click

✓ **Changing the Default Printer**
The default printer is listed at the top of the **Print** dialog box. If necessary, choose another printer from the drop-down list.

✓ **Getting Help in Dialog Boxes**
To learn more about options in dialog boxes, click the **Help** button, represented by a question mark (**?**), in the upper-right corner of the dialog box. Then click the option about which you want information.

✓ **Other Printing Alternatives**
See Part 10 for the steps to print audience handouts, speaker's notes, and an outline of your presentation.

⑤ You can print all the slides in your presentation, the slide currently displayed, or only slides you specify.

⑥ To print more than one copy of the slides, use the up-arrow button or type the number of copies.

⑦ When printing draft copies of your slides, click **Grayscale** to avoid wasting your printer's colored ink.

⑧ When you have selected the print options, click **OK**.

End Task

Task 13: Using the AutoContent Wizard to Create New Presentations

Getting Started with Professionally Designed Presentations

Do you need help deciding what topics to include in your presentation? Use the AutoContent Wizard and select from 24 presentation templates.

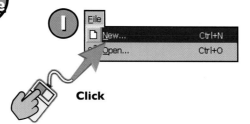

Start Here

File
New...   Ctrl+N
Open...   Ctrl+O

Click

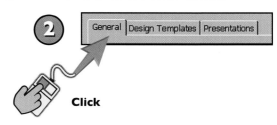

General | Design Templates | Presentations

Click

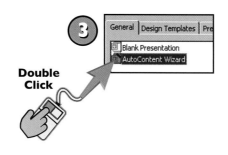

General | Design Templates | Pre
Blank Presentation
AutoContent Wizard

Double Click

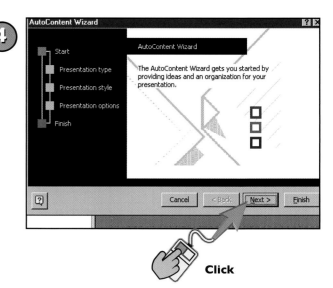

AutoContent Wizard

Start
Presentation type
Presentation style
Presentation options
Finish

AutoContent Wizard

The AutoContent Wizard gets you started by providing ideas and an organization for your presentation.

Cancel   < Back   Next >   Finish

Click

 Another Way to Access the Wizard
You can also access the wizard through the initial PowerPoint screen. Refer to Part 1, Task 1 (see Step 3).

1 Choose **File**, **New**.

2 Click the **General** tab in the New Presentation dialog box.

3 Double-click **AutoContent Wizard**.

4 Click **Next** to advance to the next step in the wizard.

Next Step

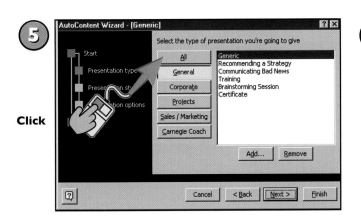

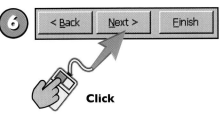

Click

Click

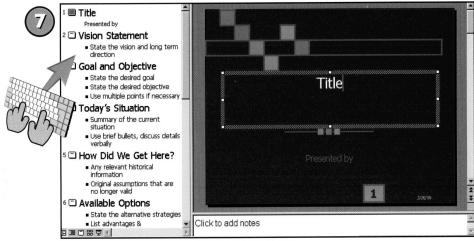

Skipping Steps in the AutoContent Wizard
Use the Roadmap in the AutoContent Wizard to quickly move to the steps you need; just click on the roadmap step to which you want to jump.

Exploring Related Features
See Part 2 for information on using the Outline pane in the Normal view. Part 3 contains steps to use bulleted lists. See Part 1, Task 6 to learn how to work with "click" placeholders.

⑤ Choose a category and presentation type from the list.

⑥ Choose **Next** to advance through each step in the wizard. Choose the **Finish** button to complete the wizard on the last step.

⑦ After you complete the wizard, the new presentation is displayed in the Normal view. Substitute your specific text for the proposed topics seen in the Outline pane.

End
Task

Task 14: Creating a New Presentation from Scratch

Creating a Blank Presentation While Working in PowerPoint

You can create new, blank presentations while you are working on other presentations in PowerPoint.

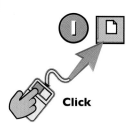

Click

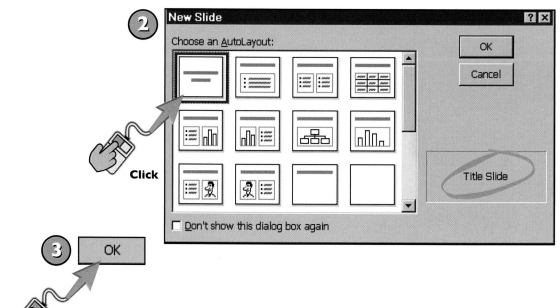

Click

Click

✓ **Adding More Slides**
Refer back to Part 1, Task 7 to learn how to add more slides to the presentation. See Part 1, Task 8 for the steps to change the slide layout.

✓ **Working with Several Open Presentations**
Use the taskbar at the bottom of the screen to switch back and forth between presentations you have open.

1 Click the **New** button on the Standard toolbar.

2 In the New Slide dialog box, choose a slide layout for the first slide in your new presentation. A description of the selected layout appears in the lower-right corner of the dialog box.

3 Click **OK**. The new presentation is created, and the first slide is displayed.

Task 15: Opening an Existing Presentation

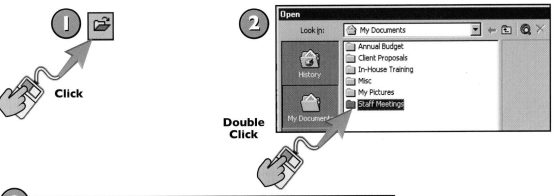

Click

Double Click

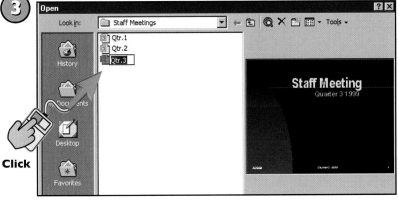

Click

Click

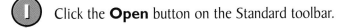

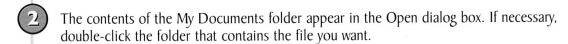

Viewing Presentations You've Already Created

You can open a PowerPoint presentation that has been previously saved. Opening a presentation is similar to opening other Windows files.

(1) Click the **Open** button on the Standard toolbar.

(2) The contents of the My Documents folder appear in the Open dialog box. If necessary, double-click the folder that contains the file you want.

(3) Click a filename to preview the first slide in the presentation. Continue to click filenames until you find the presentation you want to open.

(4) Click **Open**.

✓ **Searching for Files**
If the file you want to open is not in the My Documents folder, use the Tools, Find command in the Open dialog box to search for the file.

End Task

Introducing Clippit

One of the easiest ways to get help while using PowerPoint is to ask the Office Assistant. The default assistant is Clippit, a paperclip. If you type a few words—such as `creating charts` or `printing slides`—the Office Assistant lists several Help topics from which you can choose.

Task 16: Using Office Assistant to Get Help

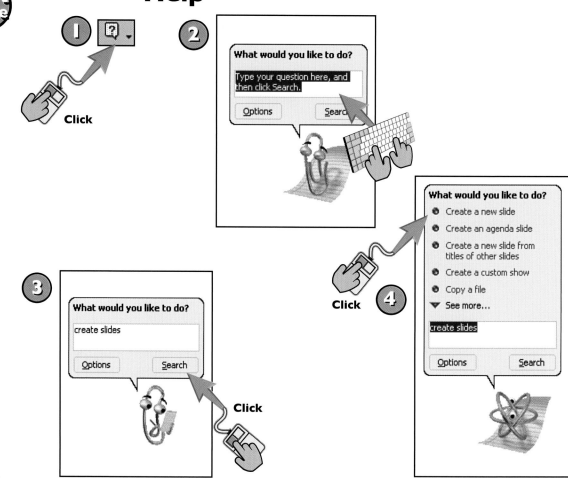

Click

1 Click the **Assistant**. If the Assistant isn't on the screen, choose **Help**, **Show the Office Assistant**.

2 In the What would you like to do? dialog box, type a few words that describe what you want to do or what you want to know about.

3 Click **Search** or press **Enter**.

4 A list of Help topics appears. Click the topic you want to view or type another description.

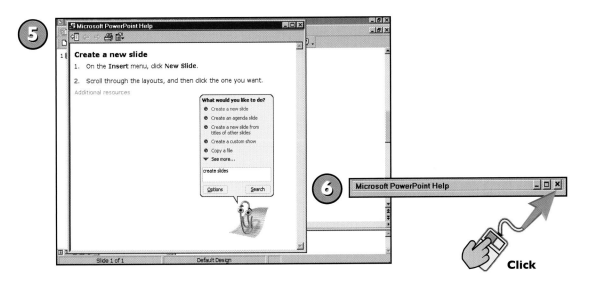

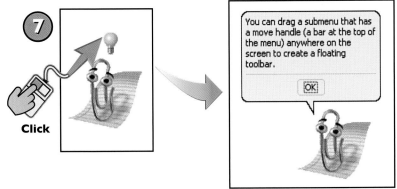

Changing the Office Assistant

If you don't like Rocky, you can choose from five other characters for the Office Assistant. Right-click **Clippit** and click **Choose Assistant**. Use the **Previous** and **Next** buttons to see the other Office Assistant characters.

Understanding the Office Assistant

Want to see the Help topics again for the last description you typed? Click the **Office Assistant**; the description is still there. Then click **Search** in the Office Assistant Help window.

Getting Help from Microsoft's Web Site

If you have access to the Internet, choose **Help, Microsoft on the Web** to see a list of PowerPoint Help topics on Microsoft's Web site.

5 You can select another help topic from the Office Assistant window or search for other topics.

6 Click the **Close** button to remove the help window.

7 When a light bulb appears next to the Office Assistant, click it to see a tip about what you're currently trying to do.

Task 17: Closing a Presentation

Clearing the Presentation Off the Screen

Closing a presentation is like storing it in a filing cabinet. Close presentations you no longer need to work with or display.

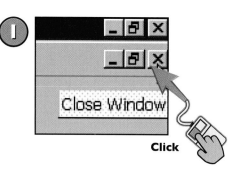

Close Window

Click

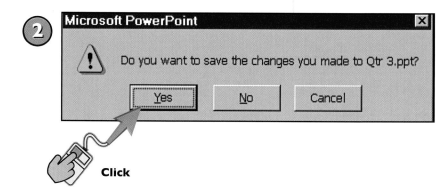

Click

✓ **Closing and Saving Files**

Choose **File, Close** to close your active presentation. If the file has not been saved previously, PowerPoint displays the **Save As** dialog box. Refer to Part 1, Task 11 for the steps to save a file.

1. Click the lower **Close** button (the one in the PowerPoint menu bar) in the upper-right corner of the PowerPoint screen.

2. If you have made changes to the presentation, PowerPoint asks you to save the changes. Click **Yes** to save the changes and close the presentation. Click **No** to close the presentation without saving the changes. Click **Cancel** to neither save nor close the presentation.

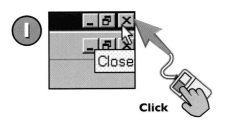

Click

Closing the PowerPoint Program

Close PowerPoint when you're finished using it. Closing PowerPoint is similar to closing any Windows program.

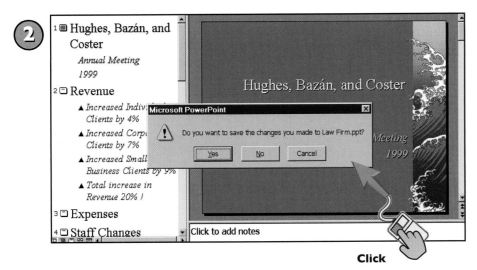

Click

✓ **Using the Menu to Close PowerPoint**
Choose **File, Exit** to close PowerPoint.

① Click the top **Close** button (the one in the PowerPoint title bar) in the upper-right corner of the PowerPoint screen.

② If you made changes to your presentations but haven't saved them, a save prompt appears for each presentation. Click **Yes** to save the changes, **No** to exit without saving the changes, or **Cancel** to cancel the command to exit and to stay in PowerPoint.

✓ **Minimizing PowerPoint**
If you want to keep PowerPoint open but need to work in another program, minimize PowerPoint instead of closing it.

Validating the Presentation Content

Part of creating effective presentations is to step back from the details and determine the overall impression your presentation will make on the audience. Is it clear? Does it flow logically?

Task 19: Tips for Improving the Content of Your Slides

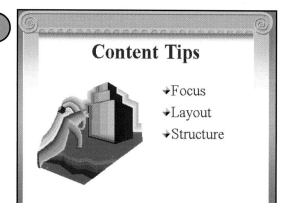

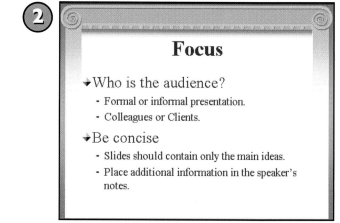

① When you have a short list of bullets, use a slide layout that combines bullets and pictures or bullets and a chart for more effective use of the slide space.

② The language and humor you use for casual, internal presentations are very different from what you use for external, formal presentations. With colleagues you can use slang and acronyms that you probably won't want to use with clients.

Layout

→ Balance
  - Use a variety of slide types.
  - Place the most important information in the upper-left corner.

→ Simplicity
  - Use blank space effectively.
  - Use graphic charts or tables or display large amounts of data.

Structure

→ Use Title Slides to introduce the major sections of your presentation.
→ Transition smoothly from topic to topic.
→ At the end of each section summarize the main points presented.

 Sometimes a graphic chart or table can convey more information than paragraphs of text. Place the most important information in the upper-left corner of the slide.

 Use the Title slide layout to introduce or conclude a topic. Make sure you present the topics in a logical order; don't jump from topic to topic.

 How Detailed Should the Slide Text Be?
It is not necessary to include paragraphs of explanations in your slides. Instead, use speaker's notes pages to write explanations for each topic you will discuss. The text on the slides should summarize the topics.

Checking the Presentation Design

The design choices you make can enhance or degrade the information you are presenting. Good text case, font type, and color choices lend essential legibility to your slides.

Task 20: Tips for Improving the Design of Your Slides

Start Here

1

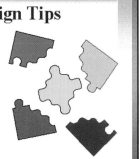

Design Tips

- Uppercase versus Mixed Case
- Sans Serif versus Serif
- Using Color Effectively

2

One of the Most Common Mistakes - Cluttered Slide

- Too many objects can make your slides difficult to interpret by the audience.
- Lengthy text and picture clips are usually the cultprits. Less is more.

3

UPPERCASE vs Mixed Case

- IT WILL TAKE YOUR AUDIENCE LONGER TO READ SLIDES THAT ARE IN ALL UPPERCASE.
- Instead, only use uppercase to EMPHASIZE specific text in your slides. Or better still, use bold or italic instead.

1 Wise font and color choices can make your slides easier to see and understand.

2 One of the most common design mistakes is adding too many objects to your slides.

3 Another mistake is to use only uppercase letters in your slides. Uppercase is harder to read than mixed case.

Next Step

Sans Serif vs Serif

→ Sans Serif fonts are best for presentation slides. Arial is a Sans Serif font.

→ Serif fonts are more difficult to read from the back of a large room. Times New Roman is a Serif font.

Choosing the Right Colors

→ People suffering from color blindness cannot distinguish red from green.

→ Avoid using similar colors next to one another, such as black with blue, or yellow with white.

4 Serif fonts look formal, but are somewhat difficult to read in a presentation. Sans serif fonts look less formal and are easier to read.

5 If you decide to change the colors of text or chart data, make sure you choose contrasting colors. Yellow text on a white slide background, for example, is difficult to see.

✅ **Changing Text Appearance**
See **Part 3, Task 12** for steps on changing the font type and text color.

✅ **Changing the Presentation Design Colors**
Choose **Format, Slide Color Scheme** to change the colors used with your presentation design.

End Task

Working with the PowerPoint Views

In Part I we worked exclusively with the Slide pane in the Normal view. Not only does the Normal view have two other panes, but other views are available in PowerPoint that you can use while designing and modifying your presentations. Part 2 introduces you to the other panes in the Normal view and to these other views and the ways in which you can use them.

The following list breaks down each view and when to use it:

- Use the Outline pane and Outline view to quickly create many slides and to show the text in each slide.

- Use the Notes pane and Notes Pages view to create printed notes, referred to as **speaker's notes**.

- The Slide Sorter view displays a miniature of each slide in the presentation. Use this view when adding transitions, timing, and animation to your slides (discussed in Part II).

- Use the Slide Show view to display a presentation to an audience, or to preview before you print copies of the presentation slides.

Tasks

Task 1: Taking Advantage of the Normal View

Using the Tri-pane View

PowerPoint's Normal (tri-pane) view provides quick access to all the key elements of a presentation.

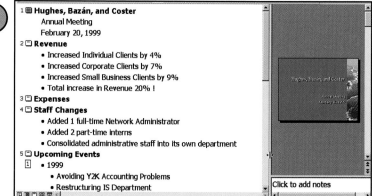

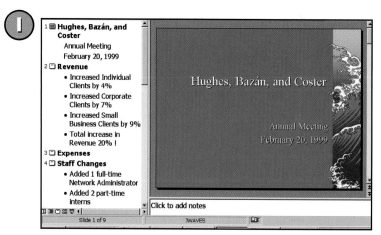

✓ **Adjusting the Panes**
When you change the size of one pane, PowerPoint automatically adjusts the size of the other panes (see Step 3). Drag the dividing line between the panes to adjust the pane size.

✓ **Adding Toolbars to the Normal View**
Right-click any toolbar to display the list of toolbars available in PowerPoint. Then click the name of the toolbar you want to display.

1 Use the Slide pane to manipulate text and add objects to individual slides.

2 Use the Drawing toolbar to add pictures, WordArt, and shapes to your slides in the Slide pane. The Drawing toolbar usually appears above the status bar.

3 The Outline pane is great for seeing the overall organization of your presentation and is useful for creating slides quickly (see Part 2, Task 2).

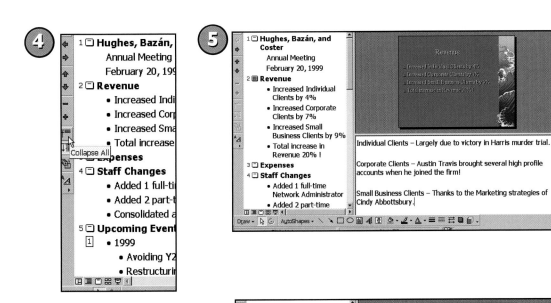

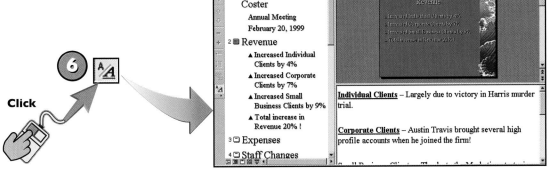

Click

4 Use the Outline toolbar to collapse and expand the outline. The Outline toolbar usually appears on the left side of the Outline pane.

5 Use the Notes pane to create printed speaker's notes for the person giving the presentation.

6 Use the Show Formatting button, found on both the Standard and Outline toolbars, to display and remove text formatting in the Outline and Notes panes.

✔ **Each Pane Scrolls Independently**
Each Normal view pane has its own set of scrollbars you can use to see additional text or slides.

✔ **Show (and Hide) Formatting Button**
The Show/Hide Formatting button (shown in Step 6) has no effect on the text in the Slide pane or on printed output.

Task 2: Using the Outline Pane to Create Slides Quickly

Use the Outline Pane to Build a Presentation

If you prefer to jot down the main topics of your presentation and fill in the details later, use the Outline pane in the Normal view.

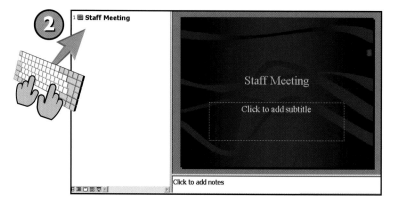

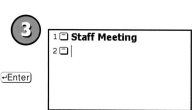

✓ **Only Text Is Visible in the Outline Pane**

The Outline pane is used primarily to create text slides, such as bulleted or numbered lists. To create graphic charts or to insert picture clips, you must use the Slide pane.

1 Click the Outline pane of the Normal view. Each slide displays a slide number and symbol.

2 Type the title for the first slide. The text appears in the Slide pane as you type in the Outline pane.

3 Press **Enter** to create the next slide.

4 Continue to create new slides by typing a title or subject, and then pressing **Enter**.

Next Step

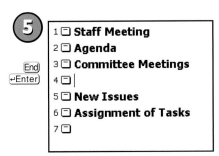

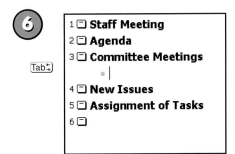

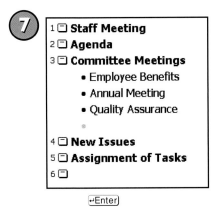

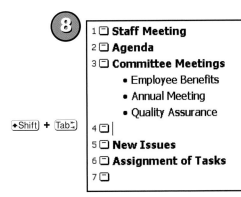

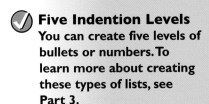

Five Indention Levels
You can create five levels of bullets or numbers. To learn more about creating these types of lists, see Part 3.

When to Use the Outline View
The Outline view is similar to the Normal view, only the emphasis is on the Outline pane instead of the Slide pane. Use the Outline view to quickly enlarge the Outline pane.

5 To insert a slide, click the slide above where you want the new slide to appear. Press **End** and then **Enter**.

6 To create a list of bullets, first create a new slide (Step 5), and then press **Tab** to indent one level.

7 Each time you press **Enter**, a new bullet appears at the same level.

8 To outdent a bullet, press **Shift+Tab**. When you outdent a first-level bullet, the symbol converts to a slide.

Preparing Presentation Notes

Each slide can have its own set of notes. Typically, you print these notes for the speaker to use during a presentation or briefing. Having printed notes ensures that you don't forget the points you want to make!

Task 3: Using the Notes Pane to Create Speaker's Notes

Start Here

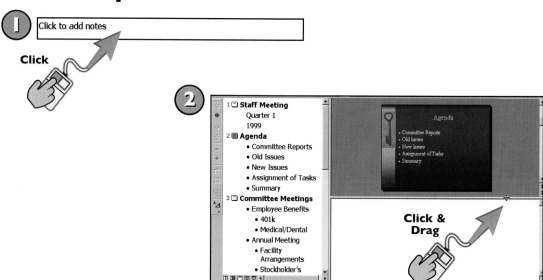

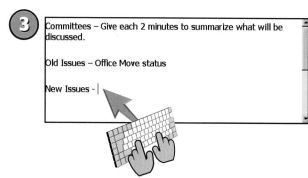

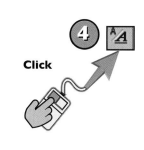

① In the Normal view's Slide pane, display the slide for which you want to create notes. Then click the **Notes** pane.

② If necessary, drag the horizontal or vertical pane dividers to adjust the size of the Notes pane.

③ Type the notes you want to associate with the active slide.

④ Click the **Show Formatting** button on either the Standard or Outline toolbar.

Next Step

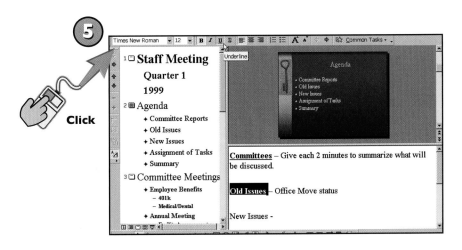

Click

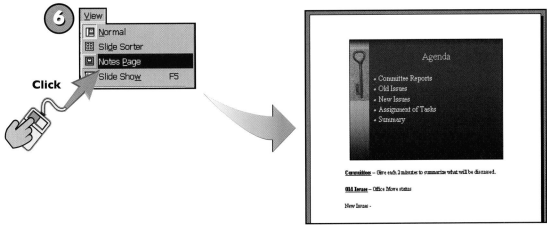

Click

⑤ Select the text and use the Formatting toolbar buttons to change the font type or size or to add bold, italic, or underline formats in the Notes pane.

⑥ Choose **View**, **Notes Page** to preview the way the speaker's notes will appear when printed.

✓ **Format the Text in Your Speaker's Notes**
Applying simple formats such as boldface or increasing the font size will make your notes more readable. This is especially useful when giving a presentation in a room where the lights are dimmed.

✓ **Be Careful Adding Bullets to Notes**
Although the Notes pane shows a space between the bullet and the note, when you print there won't be a space. Press the **Spacebar** once or twice to create spaces before typing the text. The way the notes appear in the Notes Page view is how they will appear when they are printed.

End Task

Moving Slides Around

From time to time you will need to reorder the slides in your presentation. Whether you want to move one or several slides, it's best to use the Slide Sorter view.

Task 4: Rearranging the Slide Order in the Slide Sorter View

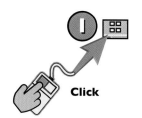

Start Here

① Click

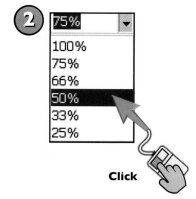

②

| 75% | ▼ |
| 100% |
| 75% |
| 66% |
| 50% |
| 33% |
| 25% |

Click

③

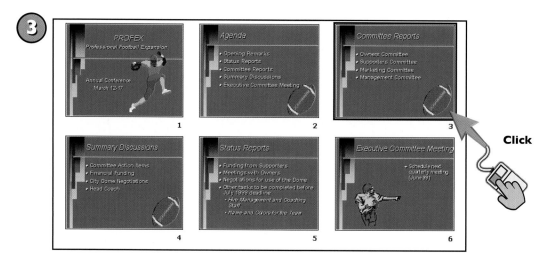

Click

✓ **Deleting Slides**
To remove unwanted slides, select the slide and press **Delete**. Choose **Edit, Undo** to recover a slide you have accidentally deleted.

① Click the **Slide Sorter View** button in the lower-left corner of the PowerPoint screen.

② To see more slides on the screen, use the **Zoom** control on the toolbar and select a lower percentage.

③ Click the slide you want to move. A heavy border appears around the slide.

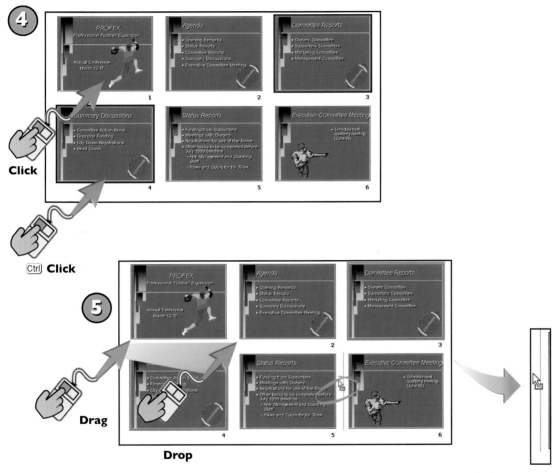

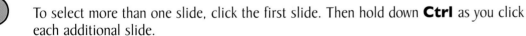

To select more than one slide, click the first slide. Then hold down **Ctrl** as you click each additional slide.

After you select all the slides to move, drag and drop the slides to the new position. A gray line indicates where you are moving the slides.

When to Use the Cut-and-Paste Commands
If the position you want to move the slides to is not visible on the screen, it is easier to use the Cut and Paste commands than to drag and drop the slides to a new position. Choose **Edit, Cut**, click the position you want the slides moved to, and choose **Edit, Paste**.

Task 5: Using the Other Views in PowerPoint

Getting Acquainted with the PowerPoint Views

Six views are available in PowerPoint for creating, enhancing, and previewing your presentations. The default view is the Normal view. You can switch among most views using the view buttons at the bottom-left corner of the PowerPoint window. You can switch to the Notes Page view only through the View menu.

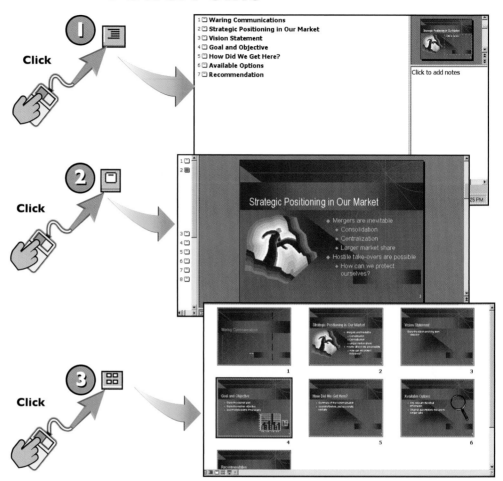

Click

Click

Click

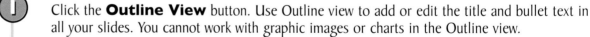

(1) Click the **Outline View** button. Use Outline view to add or edit the title and bullet text in all your slides. You cannot work with graphic images or charts in the Outline view.

(2) Click the **Slide View** button. In Slide view, you can work with the text, picture clips, and graphic charts—one slide at a time.

(3) Click the **Slide Sorter View** button. In Slide Sorter view, you can move, copy, and delete slides, but you cannot edit the slide text or work with slide objects.

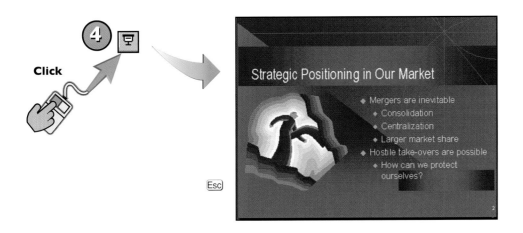

Click

Esc

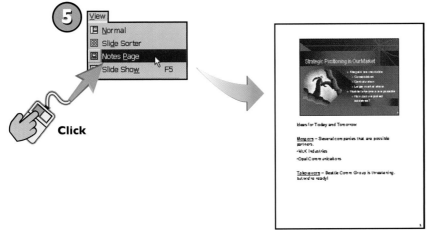

Click

Click the **Slide Show** button. Use the Slide Show view to preview how your slides will appear on an overhead or when printed. (Press the **Esc** key to exit the slide show.)

Choose **View**, **Notes Page**. Use the Notes Page view to preview how your speaker's notes will print.

✔ **Resizing Panes**
Drag the horizontal and vertical dividers to resize the panes in the Normal, Outline, and Slide views.

✔ **Slide Pane Won't Automatically Resize?**
To make the slide fit the pane, click the **Zoom** control on the Standard toolbar and choose **Fit**.

! **WARNING**
You cannot edit the slide text in the Notes Page view. This view is used to create printed speaker's notes.

End Task

Working with Text

In this part, we focus on the text components of your presentations. Along with editing, moving, copying, and deleting slide text, this part shows you how to apply formats such as bold, italic, and color to enhance the appearance of the text and how to choose from many font styles and sizes.

You also learn to create and modify bulleted and numbered lists—important elements in many slide presentations. These lists can appear by themselves or can be paired with graphic charts or picture clips in other slide layouts.

Tasks

Task 1: Creating a Bulleted List

Adding a List of Bullets to a Slide

One of the most popular types of slides in a presentation is a list of bullets. PowerPoint contains slide layouts for a single list of bullets, a double list, a list paired with a graphic chart, or a list paired with a picture clip.

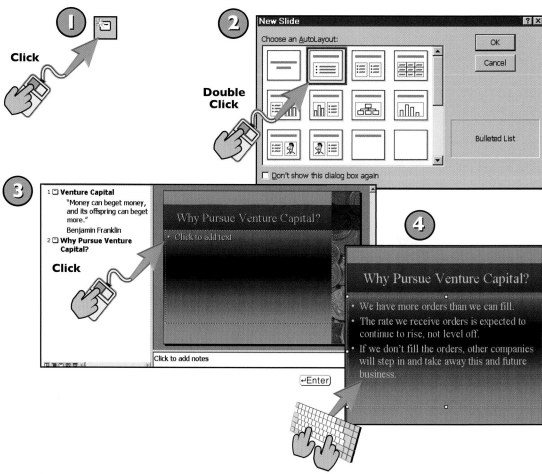

Lists with Multiple Levels

You can use up to five levels of bullets in a PowerPoint list. See Part 3, Task 3 for steps on indenting and outdenting bullets.

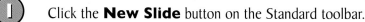

1   Click the **New Slide** button on the Standard toolbar.

2   Double-click the **Bulleted List** slide layout or one of the other layouts that includes a bulleted list.

3   When the new slide appears, click the bulleted text placeholder to begin your list of bullets.

4   Type the text for your first bullet. The text wraps to the next line if necessary. Press **Enter** for each new bullet.

Task 2: Creating a Numbered List

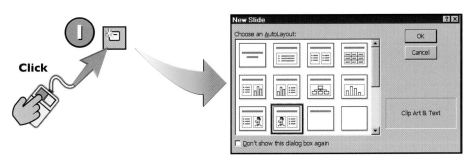

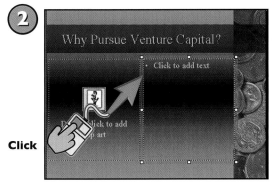

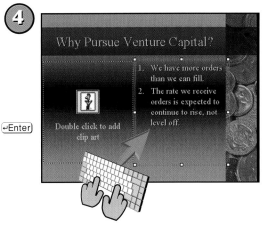

 ⏎Enter

Displaying a List of Numbered Items on a Slide

Using any of the slide layouts that contain a placeholder for bullets, you can create a list of numbered points or items on a slide.

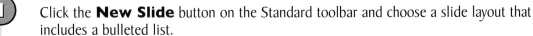

① Click the **New Slide** button on the Standard toolbar and choose a slide layout that includes a bulleted list.

② When the new slide appears, click the border of the text placeholder.

③ Click the **Numbering** button on the Formatting toolbar.

④ Type the text for your first numbered item. Press **Enter** for each new item.

✓ Using Other Numbering Styles
If you prefer to use Roman numerals or letters of the alphabet instead of the default numbering style, see Part 3, Task 6 for steps on changing the number style.

Creating Lists that Contain Indented Levels

Each slide layout that includes a bulleted list "click" placeholder is capable of displaying up to five levels of bullets or numbers. PowerPoint calls each level a "paragraph."

Task 3: Indenting and Outdenting Items in a List

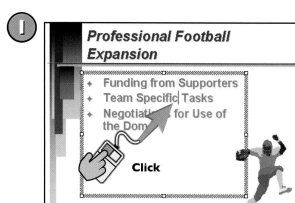

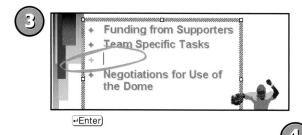

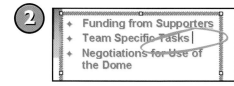

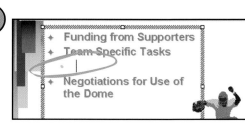

✅ **Use Tab to Indent**
Press the **Tab** key in front of an existing line to indent the paragraph one level.

① To create a new indented line, click anywhere in the line directly above where you want the new line to appear.

② Press **End** to move the cursor to the end of the line.

③ Press **Enter** to create the line.

④ Press **Tab** to indent the line one level; continue to press **Tab** to indent farther.

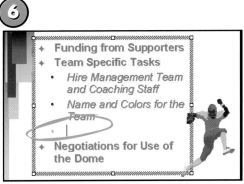

(⏎Enter)

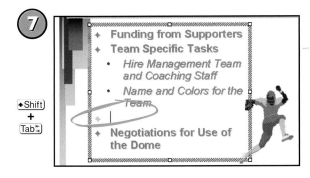

(⇧Shift)
+
(Tab⇥)

Professional Football Expansion

- ✦ Funding from Supporters
- ✦ Team Specific Tasks
  - Hire Management Team and Coaching Staff
  - Name and Colors for the Team
- ✦ Meet with Other Owners
- ✦ Negotiations for Use of the Dome

5 Type the text.

6 Each time you press **Enter**, a new symbol appears at the same level.

7 To outdent a paragraph, press **Shift+Tab**; continue to add new lines as necessary.

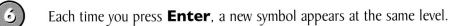

✓ **Outdenting**
In bulleted and numbered lists, you may want to move a bullet out one level. This is known as outdenting (or promoting) the bullet.

✓ **PowerPoint Uses Automatic Formatting**
If the text is too long for a line, PowerPoint automatically wraps it to the next line. If the paragraphs are so long they won't fit on the page, PowerPoint automatically reduces the font size of the text.

End Task

Task 4: Reordering a List of Bullets or Numbers

Rearranging List Paragraphs

Moving one—or even a group—of bullets or numbered items is easy with drag and drop. You can use either the Outline pane or the Slide pane to rearrange a list.

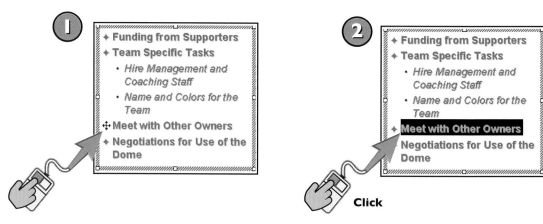

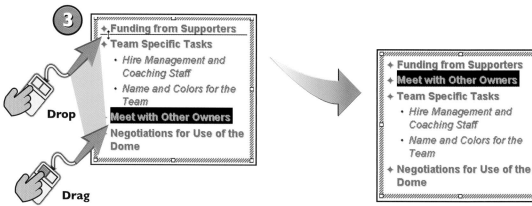

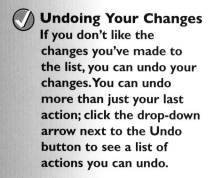

Undoing Your Changes
If you don't like the changes you've made to the list, you can undo your changes. You can undo more than just your last action; click the drop-down arrow next to the Undo button to see a list of actions you can undo.

1. Position the mouse pointer on the bullet symbol or the number; the mouse pointer becomes a four-headed arrow.

2. Click the symbol to select all the item's text.

3. Position the mouse pointer on the symbol, and then click and drag the pointer. A horizontal line appears. When you've dragged the pointer to the desired position, release the mouse button.

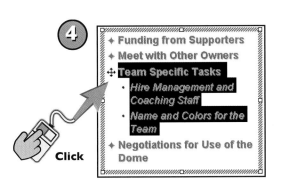

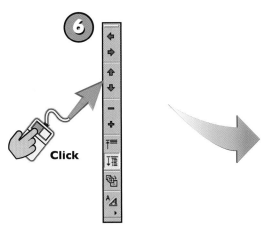

Sub-paragraphs are automatically selected when you click the main paragraph symbol.

To move an item but not any of the text indented underneath it, first drag across the item's text to highlight it.

Then click the **Move Up** or **Move Down** button on the Outline toolbar to move only the highlighted text.

✓ Displaying the Outline Toolbar

The Outline toolbar contains buttons to move text up or down in your list. To display the Outline toolbar, right-click any toolbar and choose Outline from the shortcut menu.

Changing the Shape of Several Bullets

You can change the shape of a single bullet or group of bullets on a slide.

Task 5: Modifying Bullet Symbols on a Single Slide

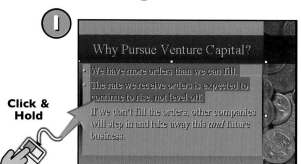

Click & Hold

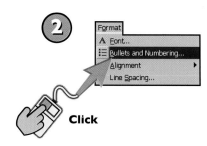

Click

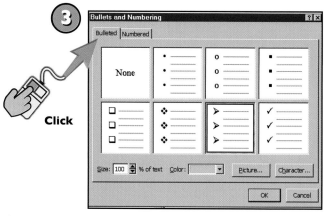

Click

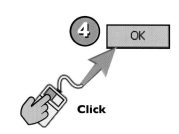

Click

✓ Changing the Bullet Size

You can enlarge or reduce the bullet's size in relation to the text's size. The Bullets and Numbering dialog box (see Step 3) contains a size option.

 Select the paragraphs with bullet symbols you want to change.

 Choose **Format**, **Bullets and Numbering**.

Click the **Bulleted** tab of the Bullets and Numbering dialog box. This tab contains a set of default symbols and options for changing the bullet size and color.

 Choose one of the default symbols, and then click **OK**.

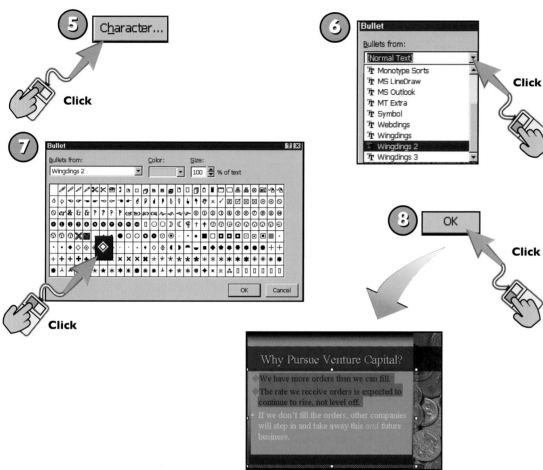

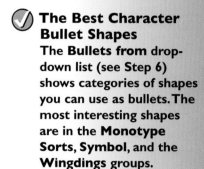

5 For a wider range of symbols, click the **Character** button.

6 Click the **Bullets from** drop-down list and choose one of the categories.

7 Choose a symbol. If desired, change the color.

8 Click **OK** to apply the symbol to your slide.

The Best Character Bullet Shapes
The **Bullets from** drop-down list (see **Step 6**) shows categories of shapes you can use as bullets. The most interesting shapes are in the **Monotype Sorts, Symbol,** and the **Wingdings** groups.

Using Pictures as Bullets
PowerPoint includes a number of colored pictures you can use as bullets. Click the **Picture** button in the Bullets and Numbering dialog box. Click a bullet and choose the first icon (**Insert Clip**) from the pop-up menu. Then close the Picture Bullets window.

Task 6: Modifying the Number Style on a Single Slide

Changing the Numeric Symbols

You can change the style of one symbol or a group of symbols in a numbered list.

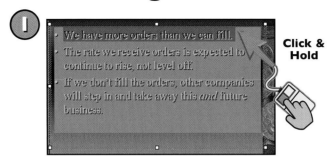

Start Here

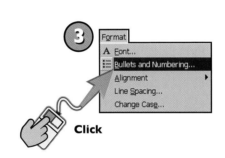

Click & Hold

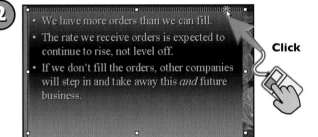

Click

Click

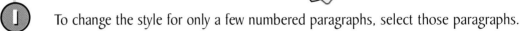

Click

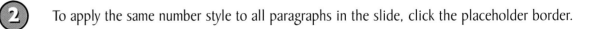

Click

Using Bullets and Numbers in Lists
You can mix bullet and number symbols in the same list; simply select the items you want to change.

To change the style for only a few numbered paragraphs, select those paragraphs.

To apply the same number style to all paragraphs in the slide, click the placeholder border.

Choose **Format**, **Bullets and Numbering**.

Click the **Numbered** tab of the Bullets and Numbering dialog box.

Next Step

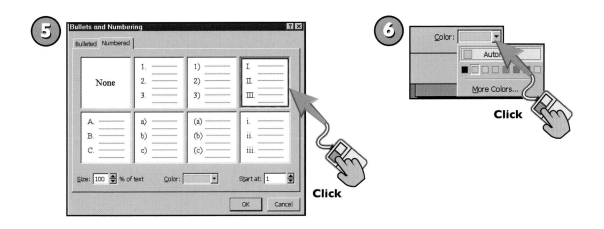

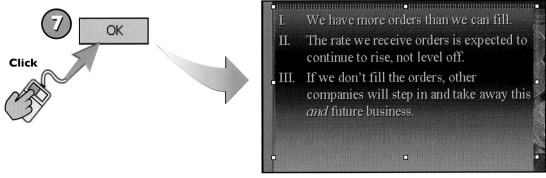

Click

5 Click the numbering style you want to apply to the selected paragraphs.

6 Choose the symbol color.

7 Click **OK** to apply the change.

✓ **Changing the Symbol Size**
You can enlarge or reduce the size of the number symbol in relation to the size of the text. The Numbered tab (see Step 5) contains a size option.

✓ **Changing the Number Style on All Slides**
Using the method described here changes the numbering style on this slide only. See Part 3, Task 7 for the steps to change the style on every slide in the presentation.

Changing the Paragraph Symbols on Every Slide

Using the Slide Master, you can apply the same bullet or number symbols to all slides and customize the symbols at each level. The Slide Master controls the symbols on slide layouts that contain a placeholder for bulleted text.

Task 7: Modifying Bullet Symbols or Number Styles on All Slides

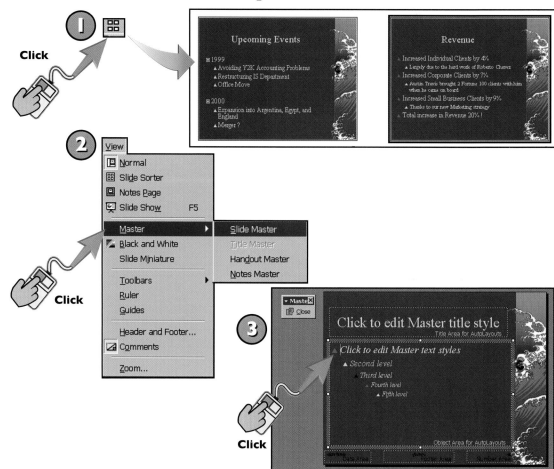

1. Click the **Slide Sorter View** button (in the button group at the lower-left corner of the PowerPoint screen) to display your slides side by side.

2. Choose **View**, **Master**, **Slide Master**.

3. The Slide Master displays, showing the five paragraph levels. Click the level for which you want to change the symbol or number style.

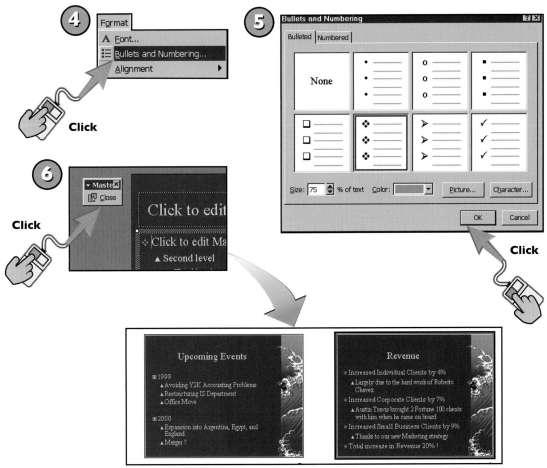

Click

Click

Click

Click

④ Choose **Format**, **Bullets and Numbering**.

⑤ Select the desired paragraph symbol, color, and size; then click **OK**. See Part 3, Tasks 5 and 6, for these steps.

⑥ The new paragraph symbol appears in the Slide Master. Click **Close** to exit the Slide Master. PowerPoint applies the new paragraph symbol to all slides.

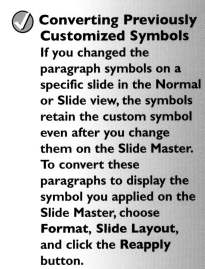

Converting Previously Customized Symbols
If you changed the paragraph symbols on a specific slide in the Normal or Slide view, the symbols retain the custom symbol even after you change them on the Slide Master. To convert these paragraphs to display the symbol you applied on the Slide Master, choose **Format, Slide Layout,** and click the **Reapply** button.

End Task

Inserting and Replacing Text in "Click" Placeholders

You can add or change the text in the title, subtitle, or bulleted list placeholders in any of your slides.

Task 8: Changing the Text in a "Click" Placeholder

Start Here

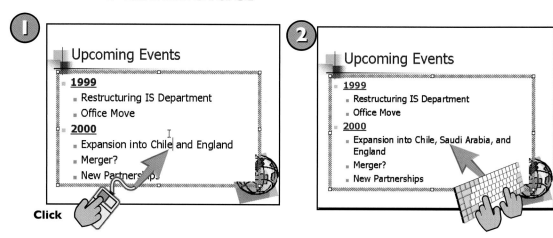

Click

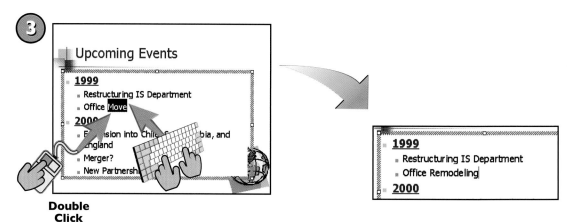

Double Click

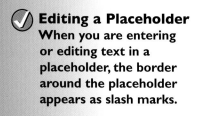
Editing a Placeholder
When you are entering or editing text in a placeholder, the border around the placeholder appears as slash marks.

① To insert text in a "click" placeholder, click the point where you want to add text. The mouse pointer becomes a capital "I" shape and a flashing cursor appears where you clicked.

② Type the text you want to add. The placeholder automatically wraps text as needed.

③ To replace a word, double-click the word to select it; then type the new word.

Next Step

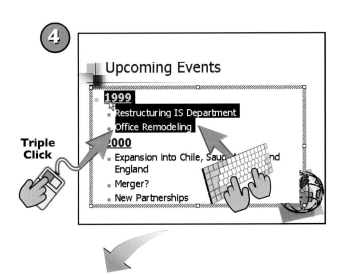

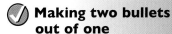

4 To change an entire bullet or paragraph, triple-click the bullet or paragraph; then type the new text.

5 If you accidentally delete the text in a "click" placeholder, click the **Undo** button.

✅ **Making two bullets out of one**
To make two bullets from one, first position the flashing cursor at the point in the text where the new bullet should begin. Then press **Enter** to move the text to the right of the flashing cursor to a new line.

✅ **Triple-clicking**
Triple-clicking text in a list highlights text in the current level and sublevels.

Deleting Words, Paragraphs, or the Entire Text in a Placeholder

The first step in removing text from a "click" placeholder is to select it. You can use both mouse and keyboard methods to select text. After you select the text, press the **Delete** key to remove it.

✓ **Deleting Text in Text Boxes**
You can remove words from a text box the same as you do from a placeholder. However, when you remove all the text in a text box, PowerPoint also deletes the text box.

Task 9: Removing Text in a "Click" Placeholder

Start Here

Double Click + Del

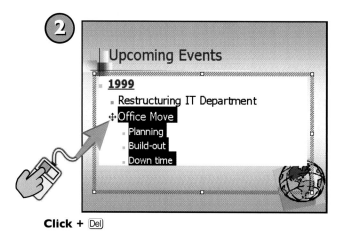

Click + Del

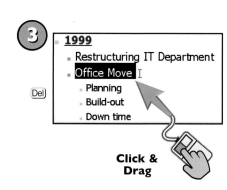

Click & Drag

1. To remove a single word in a "click" placeholder, double-click the word and press **Delete**.

2. To remove an entire bullet or numbered item, click the bullet or number symbol (the mouse changes to a 4-headed arrow) and press **Delete**.

3. To delete several words, click in front of the first word and drag across the words to select them. Then press **Delete**.

Next Step

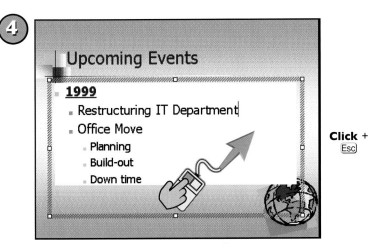

Click +
Esc

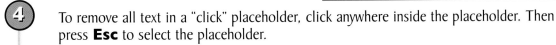

Del

4 To remove all text in a "click" placeholder, click anywhere inside the placeholder. Then press **Esc** to select the placeholder.

5 Press **Delete**. The click prompt reappears in the placeholder.

✓ **Selecting Text with the Arrow Keys**
You can use the arrow keys on the keyboard to select text. Position the flashing cursor at the beginning of the text you want to select. Then press and hold the **Shift** key while you press an arrow key. Use the right arrow key to select text to the right; use the left arrow key to select text to the left. Continue to press the arrow key until you select all the text.

Rearranging Text in a Slide

Use the **Cut**, **Copy**, and **Paste** toolbar buttons to move or copy text from one part of a slide to another or to other slides.

Task 10: Moving or Copying Text in a "Click" Placeholder

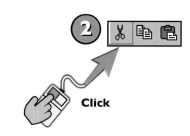

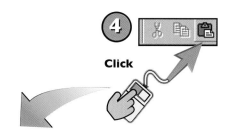

① To move text, drag the mouse pointer across the text to select it.

② Click the **Cut** button to remove the text from its current location.

③ Click to position the cursor where you want to move the text; the flashing cursor indicates the position.

④ Click the **Paste** button to move the text to the new location.

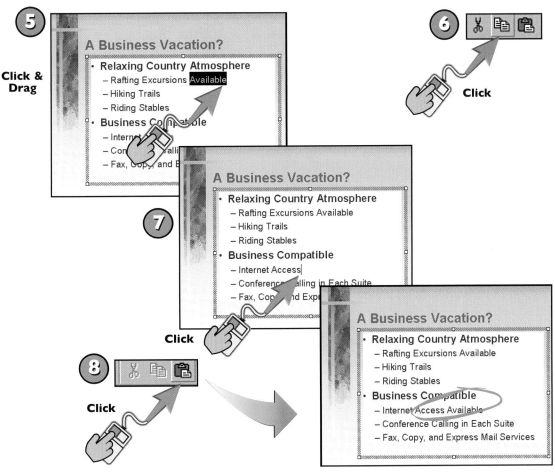

Click

Click & Drag

Click

Click

Other Methods to Select Text
You can use several methods to select text. In addition to dragging the mouse pointer across the text, you can double-click to highlight a word or click a bullet symbol to highlight an entire bullet paragraph.

Using the Edit Menu Commands
You can also use the **Cut, Copy,** and **Paste** commands in the **Edit** menu to rearrange text in a slide.

5 To copy text, first drag the mouse pointer to select the text.

6 Click the **Copy** button.

7 Click the location where you want to copy the text; the flashing cursor indicates the position.

8 Click the **Paste** button. PowerPoint copies the text to the new location.

End Task

Inserting Text Anywhere on a Slide

You can add text to a slide—separate from the placeholders—by using text boxes and AutoShapes. This kind of text is sometimes called "graphic text" or "independent text."

Task 11: Adding Independent Text to a Slide

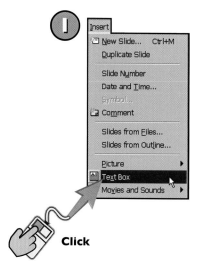

Click

Click & Drag

  Display the Drawing Toolbar
For quick access to text boxes and AutoShapes, use the Drawing toolbar. If it's not already on the screen, right-click any toolbar and click Drawing.

 Choose **Insert**, **Text Box**. The mouse pointer becomes a vertical line.

 Position the pointer where you want the text box to begin and drag to where you want it to end. A box with a flashing cursor appears.

Type the desired text.

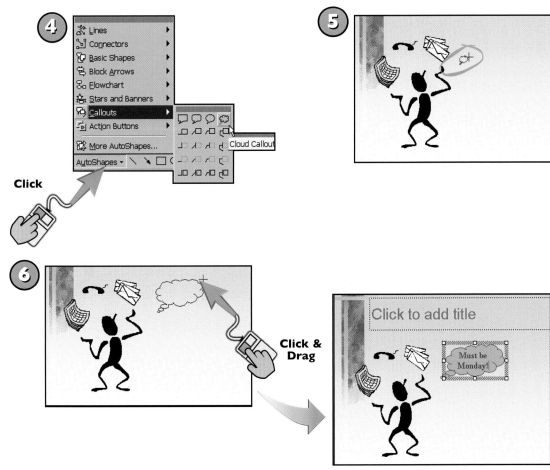

Click

**Click &
Drag**

Using AutoShapes
In addition to the callouts, you can add text to many other shapes. Draw the shape and, with the shape selected, type the text.

Text Alignment
By default, text in a text box is left-aligned and text in an AutoShape is centered. Choose **Format, Alignment** to change the alignment.

Formatting Text
See Part 3, Task 12 for information about formatting the text font, size, and color.

See Part 3, Task 13 for information about applying formats such as bold and italic.

④ Choose **AutoShapes** from the Drawing toolbar. Choose a shape from one of the categories.

⑤ The mouse pointer becomes a large plus sign (crosshairs). Position the mouse pointer where the shape is to start.

⑥ Click and drag to create the AutoShape. Type the desired text.

Formatting the Slide Text

You can greatly alter your slides' appearance by changing the text's font and size. You can also add color to your text. Each presentation has a set of eight coordinating colors; you can quickly apply any of them to your text. Or you can select any color from the color wheel.

Task 12: Changing the Font, Size, and Color of Text

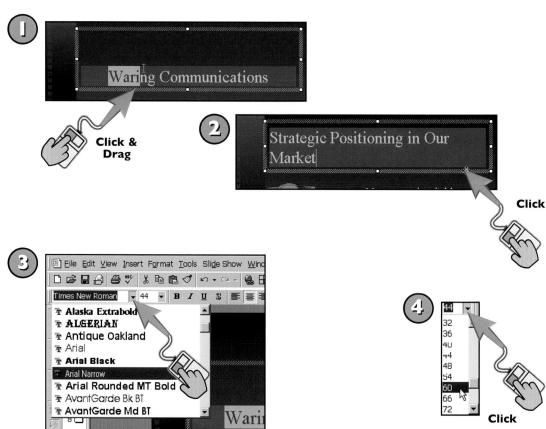

✓ **Applying a Presentation Design**
If you don't remember what a presentation design is, see Part 1, Task 10.

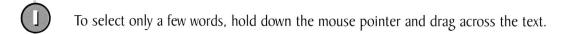

1. To select only a few words, hold down the mouse pointer and drag across the text.

2. To select all the text in a placeholder or text box, click the border. The border changes to slash marks.

3. To change the font, click the **Font** drop-down arrow and choose a font. Scroll to see more fonts.

4. To change the font size, click the **Font Size** drop-down arrow and choose the size. Scroll to see more sizes.

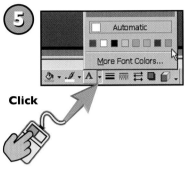

Click

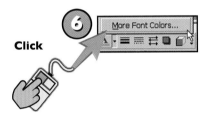

Click

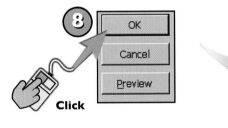

Click

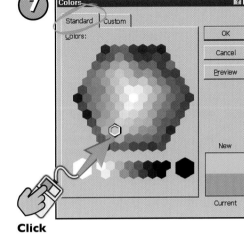

Click

Click

⑤ To change the font color, click the **Font Color** drop-down arrow on the Drawing toolbar and choose one of the presentation design colors.

⑥ To select a different color, choose **More Font Colors**.

⑦ On the Standard tab, click a color from the color wheel.

⑧ Click **OK**. PowerPoint applies the new color to the text.

✓ **Editing Independent Text**
You must use the Slide view or the Normal view's Slide pane to change independent text—that is, text outside a "click" placeholder.

✓ **Custom Font Sizes**
If the font size you want does not appear on the list, type the size in the drop-down box and press **Enter**.

End Task

Enhancing Text Through Formatting

You can use several methods to change the way text appears on your slides. You can apply formatting such as bold and italic, using buttons on the Formatting toolbar or through the Format menu.

Task 13: Applying Bold, Italic, Underline, and Shadow Formatting to Text

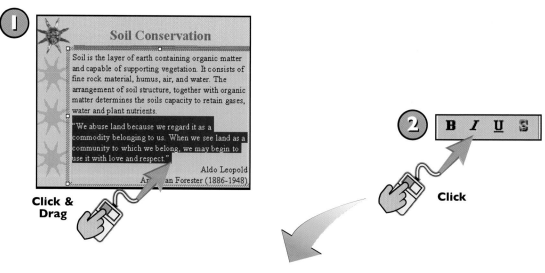

Click & Drag

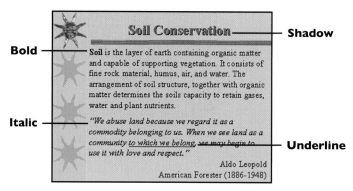

Click

Bold

Shadow

Italic

Underline

✓ **Selecting the Text Object**

To apply the same formatting to all the text in a "click" placeholder, text box, or AutoShape—click anywhere in the text. Press **Esc** to select the text object, and then apply the formatting.

① Select the text you want to change by dragging the mouse pointer across the text.

② You can quickly apply bold, italic, underline, and shadow text formatting using the buttons on the Formatting toolbar.

Task 14: Applying Superscript, Subscript, and Emboss Formatting to Text

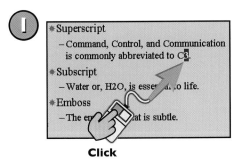

Click

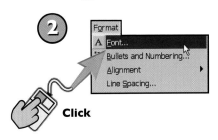

Click

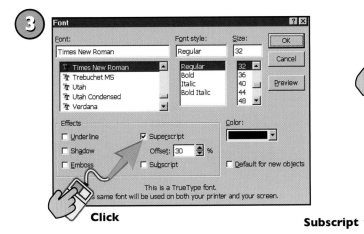

Click

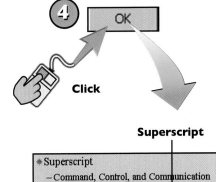

Click

Superscript

* Superscript
  - Command, Control, and Communication is commonly abbreviated to C^3.
* Subscript
  - Water or, H_2O, is essential to life.
* Emboss
  - The emboss format is subtle.

Subscript

Emboss

Using Special Formatting

PowerPoint includes formatting options to create superscripts, subscripts, and embossing. You can access these formats through the Format menu.

 Superscript and Subscript Offset
In the Font dialog box (see Step 3) there is an option to change the percentage of offset. Higher percentages move the superscript and subscript farther away from the other text.

1. Select the text you want to format.

2. Choose **Format**, **Font** from the menu bar.

3. Use the Font dialog box to apply **Superscript**, **Subscript**, and **Emboss** formats to your text.

4. Click **OK**. The formatting is applied to your text.

Adding Picture Clips, WordArt, and Drawings to Slides

PowerPoint contains many options for enlivening your presentations, including the use of images and drawings.

Pictures include colorful illustrations, symbols, cartoons, and photographs. Many picture clip images are installed with PowerPoint. Additional picture clips can be found on the Microsoft Office CD or on Microsoft's Web site.

WordArt is a feature that curves or angles the text of words or phrases. WordArt also adds special colors and shadows to the text.

You can also create a wide range of shapes in PowerPoint, such as starbursts, callout boxes, and flowchart symbols, by choosing **AutoShapes** from the Drawing toolbar.

Tasks

Task 1: Adding a Picture Clip to a Single Slide

Using Image Clips on Slides

One way to improve the appearance of a slide is to add a picture. You can add picture clips to any slide, even if it doesn't have a placeholder for a clip image.

Start Here

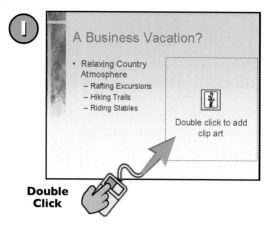

Double Click

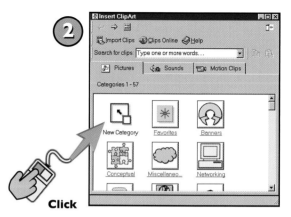

Click

Click

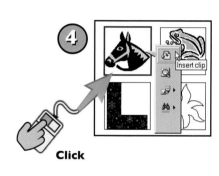

Click

✓ **Modifying Picture Clip Objects**
See Part 5, Tasks 2 and 3 to learn more about moving and resizing slide objects.

1 If the slide has a picture clip placeholder, double-click the placeholder to see the Clip Gallery.

2 Choose a category; **scroll** to see additional categories.

3 From the set of clips that appears, click to select a clip. You might have to scroll to see all the images.

4 From the pop-up menu that appears on the clip, click the first option, **Insert Clip**. The picture clip appears in the placeholder on the slide.

Next Step

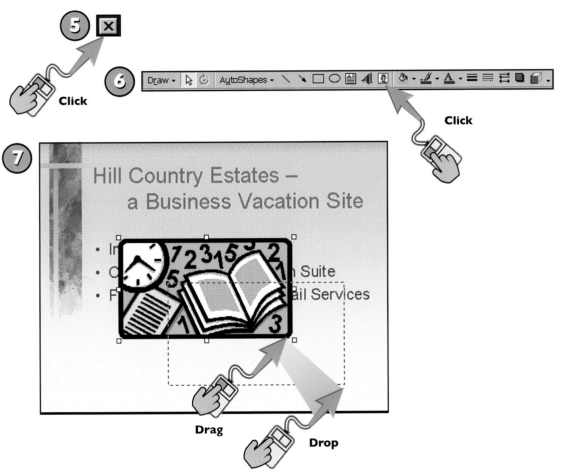

Click

Click

Hill Country Estates –
a Business Vacation Site

Drag

Drop

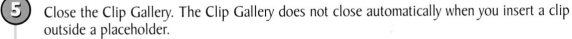

5) Close the Clip Gallery. The Clip Gallery does not close automatically when you insert a clip outside a placeholder.

6) If the slide does not have a clip placeholder, click the **Insert Clip Art** button on the Drawing toolbar to access the Clip Gallery. Repeat steps 2-5.

7) Because no placeholder is on this slide, the clip is placed in the middle of the slide. Use drag-and-drop to move the image.

✓ **Finding Additional Clips**
You can locate more picture clips on the Microsoft Web site. In the Clip Gallery, click **Clips Online** on the **Clip Gallery** toolbar. The Clip Gallery Live site appears.

Task 2: Adding the Same Picture Clip to All Slides

Placing a Clip Image on the Slide Master

If you want the same picture clip to appear on all slides, you can add the clip to the Slide Master. Clips you add to the Slide Master appear on all slides except those that have a title layout.

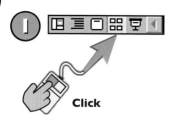

Start Here

① **Click**

② 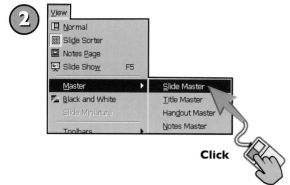 **Click**

③  **Click**

④ 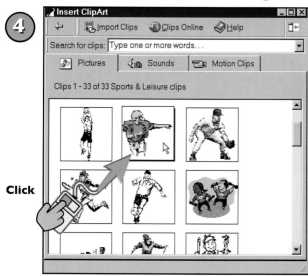 **Click**

① Switch to the **Slide Sorter View**.

② Choose **View**, **Master**, **Slide Master**.

③ Click the **Insert Clip Art** button on the Drawing toolbar.

④ The Clip Gallery opens. Select a category and a clip you want to add to the Slide Master.

Next Step

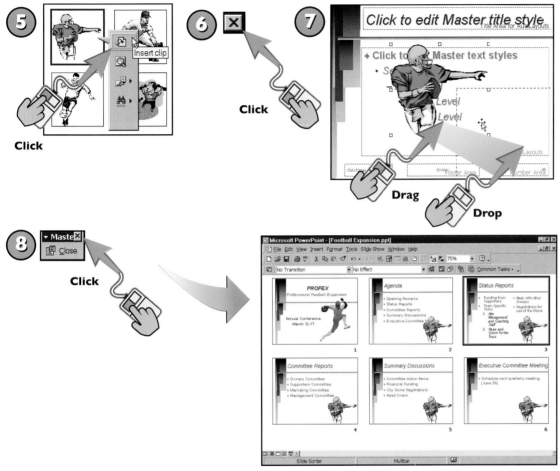

Click

Click

Drag

Drop

Click

⑤ From the pop-up that appears on the clip, click the first option, **Insert clip**.

⑥ Close the Clip Gallery.

⑦ Drag and drop the image to the desired location on the Slide Master; resize the clip as necessary.

⑧ Click the **Close** button to close the Slide Master. The image appears on all slides, except those using the title slide layout.

✓ **Modifying or Removing Clips**
You must display the Slide Master to modify or remove the picture clip.

✓ **Moving and Resizing Clips**
See Part 5, Tasks 2 and 3 to learn more about moving and resizing clip images.

Task 3: Recoloring Picture Clips

Changing the Default Colors of a Picture Clip Image

If you don't like the colors on the picture clip you want to use, change them!

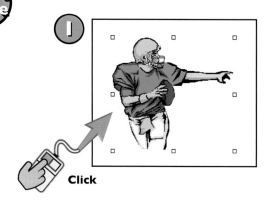

Start Here

Click

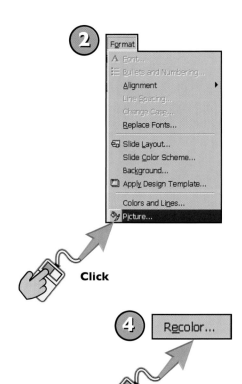

Click

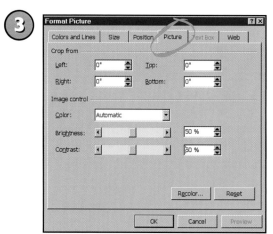

Click

✓ **Making Sure the Clip Is Selected**
When you click a picture clip, a set of selection handles appears around the image, indicating it is selected.

Click the clip you want to recolor. Selection handles appear indicating that you selected the clip.

Choose **Format**, **Picture**. The Format Picture dialog box appears.

Click the **Picture** tab.

Click the **Recolor** button on the **Picture** tab.

Next Step

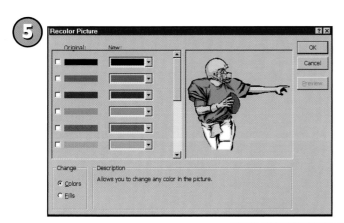

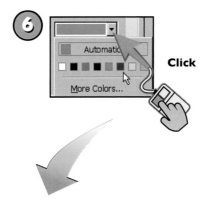

Click

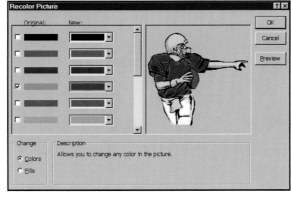

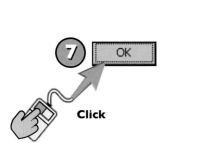

Click

⑤ The Recolor Picture dialog box shows a column indicating the original color and a column where you can select a new color.

⑥ Click the drop-down arrow next to the color you want to change. The preview automatically illustrates how the color changes will appear on the picture clip.

⑦ Click **OK** to accept the changes in the Recolor Picture dialog box. Click **OK** again to exit the Format Picture dialog box.

✅ **Identifying All the Picture Colors**
Sometimes you may have to *scroll* in the Recolor Picture dialog box to see all the colors used in the clip.

✅ **Selecting a New Clip Color**
When you click a drop-down arrow to change a color, the eight default colors that are part of the presentation design appear, along with the More Colors button. Choose **More Colors** to display a dialog box with two tabs. Choose the **Standard** tab to select a new color from a color wheel.

Task 4: Adding WordArt to a Slide

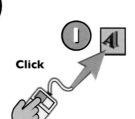

Start Here

Using WordArt to Enhance Your Slides

Another way to liven up slides is with WordArt. You often see WordArt effects on flyers or bulletin board notices.

Click

1

2

Click

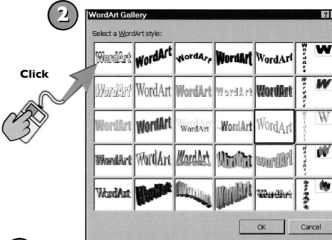

3

Click

OK

4

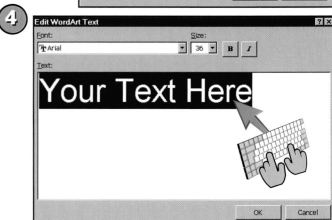

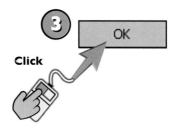

Modifying WordArt Objects

You can modify WordArt styles. See Part 4, Task 5 for steps on changing WordArt shape, direction, and color.

1 Click the **WordArt** button on the Drawing toolbar.

2 Choose the style you want for the WordArt. The styles include shape, direction, shadow, and color.

3 Click **OK**. The Edit WordArt Text dialog box appears.

4 Type the text you want for the WordArt.

Next Step

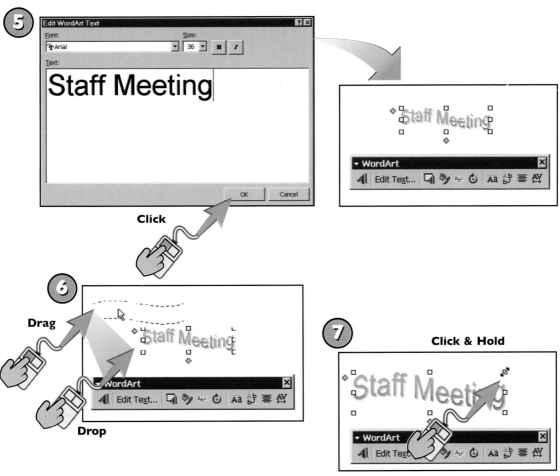

Click

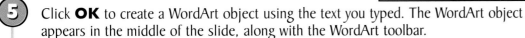

Drag

Drop

Click & Hold

5 Click **OK** to create a WordArt object using the text you typed. The WordArt object appears in the middle of the slide, along with the WordArt toolbar.

6 Drag and drop from the middle of the object to move it.

7 Drag a corner selection handle to resize the WordArt object.

✓ **Adjusting WordArt Objects**
See Part 5, Tasks 2 and 3 to learn more about moving and resizing objects.

End Task

Task 5: Changing the WordArt Style

Altering the Appearance of WordArt Objects

You can easily change the style or shape used for the WordArt by using the buttons on the WordArt toolbar.

Click

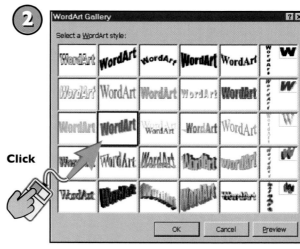

Click

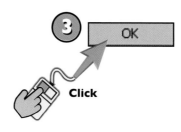

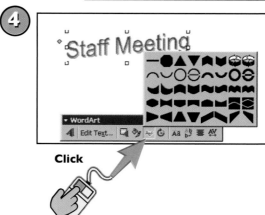

Click

Click

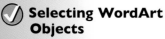

✓ Selecting WordArt Objects

To select the WordArt object, make sure the mouse pointer is a four-headed arrow before you click the object.

1. With the WordArt object selected, click the **WordArt Gallery** button on the WordArt toolbar.

2. Select a new style from the Gallery.

3. Click **OK** to apply the new WordArt style.

4. Click the **WordArt Shape** button. Then select a different shape for the display of the words.

Task 6: Editing the WordArt Text

Double Click

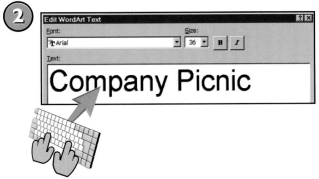

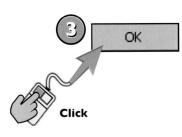

Click

Change or Edit the Text in a WordArt Object

You can quickly modify or format the WordArt text by double-clicking the WordArt object.

(1) Position the mouse pointer over the WordArt object. When the pointer changes to a four-headed arrow, double-click the object to open the Edit WordArt Text dialog box.

(2) Type the new text. Use the **Font** and **Size** drop-down boxes or the **Bold** and **Italic** buttons to format the text.

(3) Click **OK** to apply the changes to the WordArt text.

Editing WordArt Text
You can use common Windows editing techniques in the text area of the Edit WordArt Text dialog box. You can double-click to highlight a word, for example, or use the backspace key to delete one character to the left of the flashing cursor.

Task 7: Drawing Shapes on a Slide

Adding Lines, Arrows, and Other Shapes to Your Slides

PowerPoint has a Drawing toolbar that contains tools you can use to create and enhance drawn objects. The Drawing toolbar is located at the bottom of the PowerPoint window.

Start Here

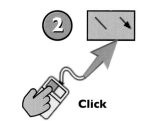
Click

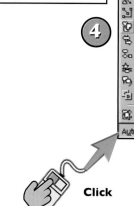

Click & Hold

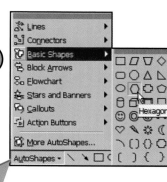
Click

Removing Unwanted Objects
If you make a mistake while drawing an object, simply select it, press the **Delete** key, and try again!

1. The Drawing toolbar is the starting point for drawing lines, arrows, and shapes.

2. From the Drawing toolbar, click either the **Line** or the **Arrow** button, depending on which object you want to draw.

3. Drag the mouse pointer from the beginning of the line or arrow to the end point.

4. To draw an AutoShape, start by selecting a shape from one of the groups listed on the **AutoShape** menu.

Next Step

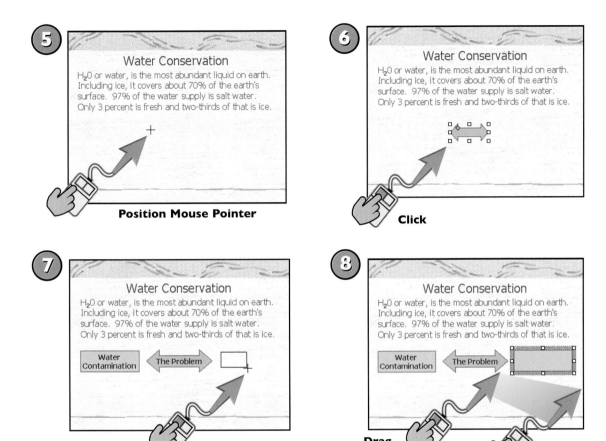

Position Mouse Pointer

Click

Click & Hold

Drag

Drop

5 One way to draw a shape is to position the mouse pointer where you want the shape to begin.

6 Click once to draw a sample of the shape. Resize the shape by dragging a selection handle.

7 Alternatively, you can click and hold the mouse pointer to start drawing the shape.

8 Drag in the direction where you want the shape to end; release the mouse button when the shape looks the way you want it.

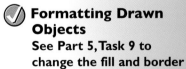

Formatting Drawn Objects
See Part 5, Task 9 to change the fill and border color of drawn objects.

End Task

Working with Slide Objects

Any item you can select on a slide is considered a slide *object*. This includes "click" placeholders, independent text boxes, picture clips, and drawings. The way you manipulate slide objects is similar, regardless of the type of object; that is, you move and resize a text object the same way that you move and resize picture clips.

In this part, you learn how to rearrange objects by moving, aligning, layering, and grouping. Additionally, this part shows you how to format, resize, copy, and delete slide objects.

Tasks

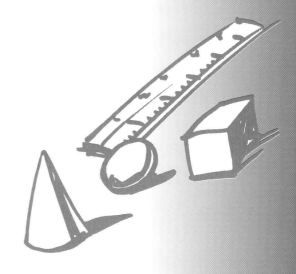

Task 1: Selecting Objects

Selecting Text and Image Objects

Before you can move, copy, resize, or delete an object, you must first select it. The procedures for selecting a text object are slightly different from those for selecting an image object.

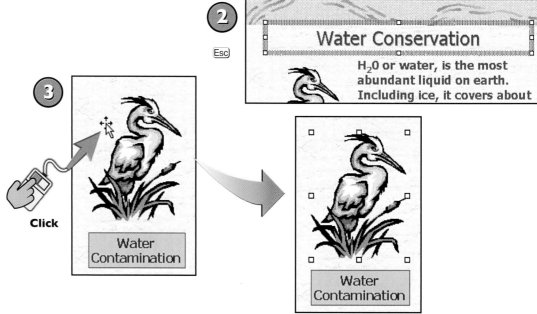

✓ **Selecting Multiple Objects**

To select more than one object, click the first object. Then press **Shift** and click each additional object you want to select.

① To select a text object, position the mouse pointer inside the text object. The pointer changes to an "I" shape or a thin plus sign. Click once.

② Press **Esc**. A set of selection handles appears around the text object, indicating it is selected. The border around the object changes to a thick band of dots.

③ To select image objects, position the mouse pointer over the object. The pointer changes to a four-headed arrow. Click once. A set of selection handles appears around the object, indicating it is selected.

Task 2: Moving Slide Objects

1 Click & Hold

3 Click & Hold

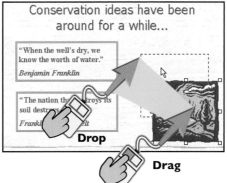

2 Drag
Drop

4 Drop
Drag

Rearranging Selected Objects

You can use drag and drop to move selected text or image objects on your slides.

 Selecting Slide Objects
See Part 5, Task 1 to learn how to select text and image objects.

 Moving Objects to Other Slides
To move an object from one slide to another slide, see Part 5, Task 5.

1 To move a selected text object, position the pointer on the object border—but not on a selection handle.

2 Hold down the mouse button and drag to move the object. Release the mouse button to drop the object in its new location.

3 To move a selected image object, position the pointer over the object.

4 Hold down the mouse button and drag to move the object. Release the mouse button to drop the object in its new location.

Task 3: Resizing Slide Objects

Altering the Size and Shape of Slide Objects

You can enlarge a slide object by dragging a selection handle away from the opposite corner. To shrink the object, drag toward the opposite corner.

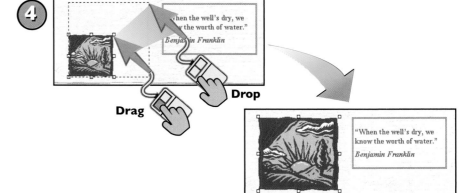

① WARNING

If you attempt to resize an image by using the top, bottom, or side selection handles, the image becomes distorted. You can avoid this by always resizing from a corner selection handle.

① To resize a text object, click anywhere on the text object.

② Drag the object by any of its selection handles. A dashed outline indicates the new dimensions.

③ To resize an image object, select it and position the mouse pointer on a corner selection handle.

④ Drag the mouse pointer to resize the image.

Task 4: Copying Slide Objects

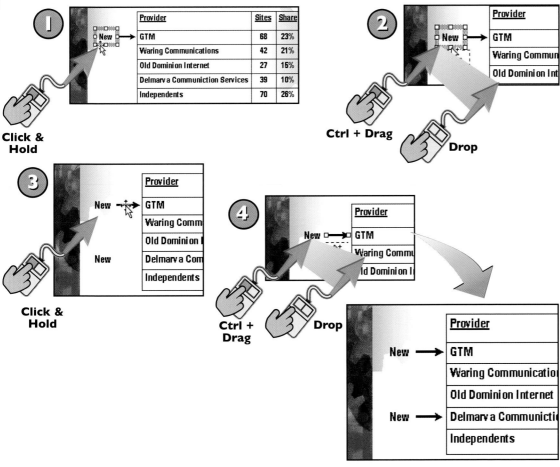

Making Copies of Objects on Your Slides

It is often easier to copy an object than to try to create an identical object from scratch. If you want a new object that is similar to one that already exists in your slide, copy the object and modify the copy. The key to copying an object is to make sure the mouse pointer is a four-headed arrow.

① Position the mouse pointer on the border of the selected text object—but not on a selection handle.

② Hold the **Ctrl** key as you drag and drop to create the copy. A plus sign appears to indicate you are creating a copy.

③ To copy an image object, position the mouse pointer over the object.

④ Hold **Ctrl** as you drag and drop to create the copy.

Copying Objects to Other Slides
To copy an object from one slide to another, see Part 5, Task 5.

Rearranging and Copying Objects Between Slides

The Cut, Copy, and Paste buttons on the Standard toolbar make it easy to move or copy objects from one slide to another.

Task 5: Moving or Copying Objects to Other Slides

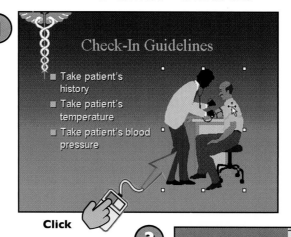

Start Here

Click

Click

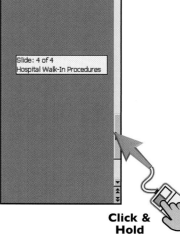

Slide: 4 of 4
Hospital Walk-In Procedures

Click & Hold

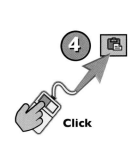

Click

✓ **Moving and Copying Objects to Other Presentations**
Use these same procedures to move or copy objects to slides in other presentations. In Step 3, open the other presentation. Use the **Window** menu to switch between the source and target presentations.

(1) Click to select the object you want to move or copy.

(2) If you want to move the object, click the **Cut** button. If you want to copy the object, click the **Copy** button.

(3) Drag the scroll box on the vertical scrollbar to find the slide into which you want to paste the object.

(4) Click the **Paste** button on the Standard toolbar.

End Task

Task 6: Deleting Slide Objects

Start Here

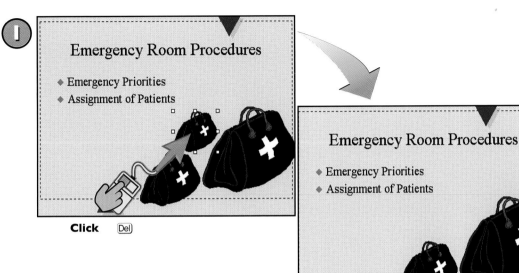

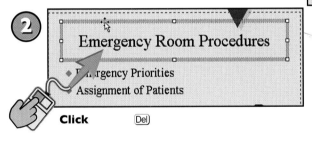

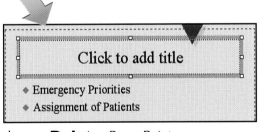

Removing Objects from Slides

You can delete unwanted objects from a slide by selecting the object and pressing the **Delete** key. If you don't remember how to select objects, see Part 5, Task 1.

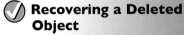
Recovering a Deleted Object
If you accidentally delete an object, choose **Edit, Undo** to recover the object.

Deleting Placeholders
To delete an empty "click" placeholder, select it and press **Delete**.

① To delete an image or a text box, select the object and press **Delete**. PowerPoint removes the object from the slide.

② To delete the text in a "click" placeholder, select the placeholder and press **Delete**. The text in the placeholder is removed but the placeholder remains. Empty placeholders do not print or display when you run the slide show.

Lining Up Objects on Your Slides

The **Drawing** toolbar contains many options for aligning objects on your slides. Among other alignment choices, you can left-align, right-align, or center objects, and you can distribute them evenly in a horizontal or vertical row.

Task 7: Aligning and Distributing Slide Objects

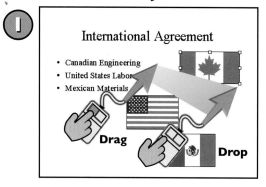

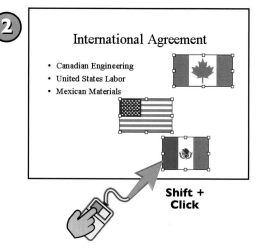

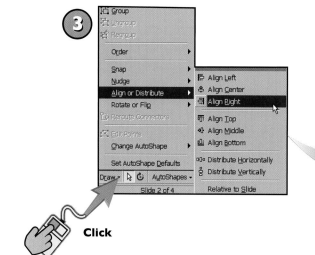

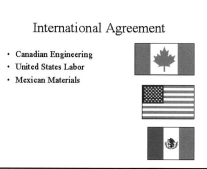

✓ **Displaying the Drawing Toolbar**
If the **Drawing** toolbar is not displayed, choose **View, Toolbars,** and then select **Drawing.**

① Drag and drop one of the objects to the position where you want all the objects to line up.

② Press **Shift** and click each additional object. Each selected object will display selection handles.

③ From the Drawing toolbar, choose **Draw, Align or Distribute**. Then choose the alignment option you need.

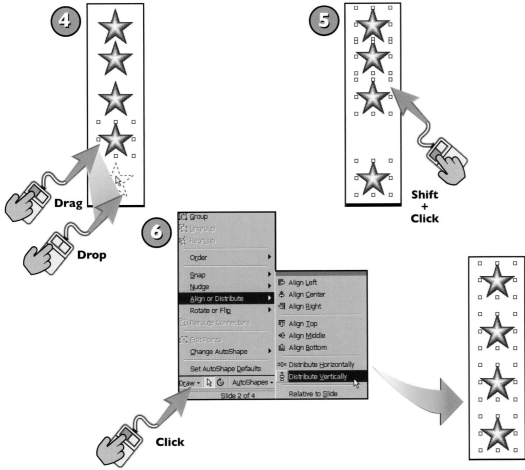

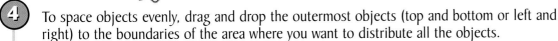

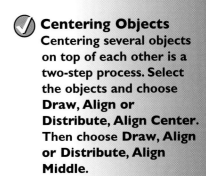

To space objects evenly, drag and drop the outermost objects (top and bottom or left and right) to the boundaries of the area where you want to distribute all the objects.

Press **Shift** and click to select all the objects you want to distribute.

From the Drawing toolbar, choose **Draw**, **Align or Distribute**. Then choose the distribution you want—**Distribute Horizontally** or **Distribute Vertically**.

✓ **Centering Objects**
Centering several objects on top of each other is a two-step process. Select the objects and choose **Draw, Align or Distribute, Align Center**. Then choose **Draw, Align or Distribute, Align Middle**.

Task 8: Formatting Text Objects

Applying a Background Color and Border to Text Objects

You can enhance any text object by changing its formatting. Use color and line options to add a colorful background and border to your object.

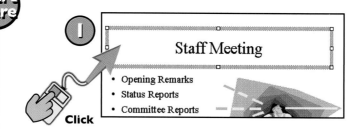

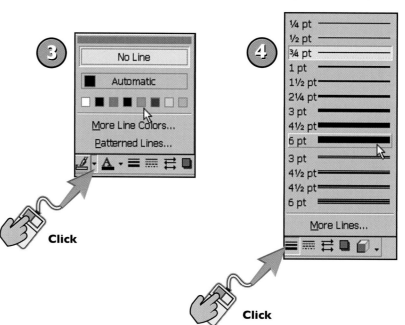

Start Here

Click

Click

Click

Click

✓ **Displaying the Drawing Toolbar**
By default, the Drawing toolbar appears at the bottom of the PowerPoint screen. If the toolbar is not displayed, choose **View, Toolbars, Drawing**.

(1) Select the text object you want to enhance.

(2) To apply a background color behind the text, click the drop-down arrow to the right of the **Fill Color** button and choose a color.

(3) Most text objects do not display a border around the object. If you click the drop-down arrow on the **Line Color** button and choose a color, you can add a line around the text object.

(4) To change the thickness of the line or to display alternative styles, click the **Line Style** button and choose a style.

Next Step

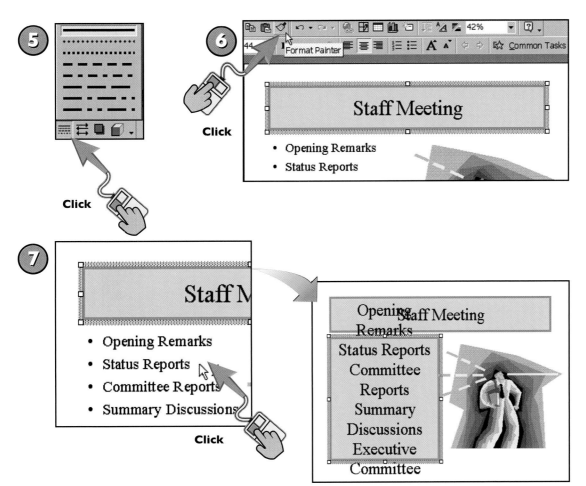

⑤ To apply a dashed or dotted line style, click the **Dash Line** button and choose a dash style.

⑥ To copy attributes such as line and fill color from one object to another, select the object containing the attributes you want to copy and click the **Format Painter** button.

⑦ Position the mouse pointer on the object where you want to apply the attributes and click. PowerPoint applies all the attributes from the original object. See the "Adjusting Text in a Text Box" tip.

✔ **Coloring Slide Objects**
See Part 5, Task 9 for additional fill-color (background) options you can use with slide objects.

✔ **Adjusting Text in a Text Box**
If the text is too long to fit in a text box, you can either change the text font size or enlarge the box. See Part 3, Task 12 for steps to change the font size. See Part 5, Task 3 to learn how to resize objects.

End Task

Task 9: Formatting Drawn Objects

Applying a Background Color and Border to Drawn Objects

You can enhance any object you draw by changing its color and line attributes.

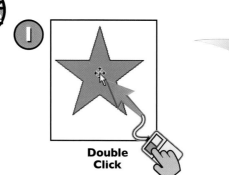

Start Here

Double Click

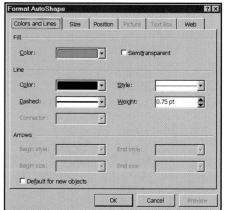

✓ **Setting the Default Formatting for AutoShapes**

The Format AutoShape dialog box contains an option to set the current formatting as the default for any new AutoShape objects drawn in the active presentation. This will save you a lot of time if you plan to draw more objects and want them to have the same formatting attributes.

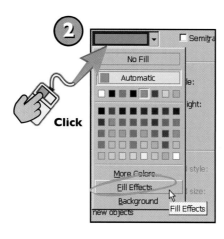

Click

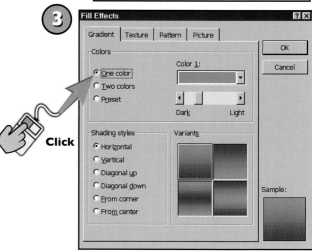

Click

Double-click the object you want to enhance. If the object is a line or arrow, the Format Object dialog box appears. Otherwise, the Format AutoShape dialog box appears.

To change the fill color, choose one of the displayed colors or select any color by choosing **More Colors**. Click **Fill Effects** to fill the object with a gradient, a texture, a pattern, or a picture.

In the Fill Effects dialog box, select the **Gradient** tab and click the **One Color** option.

Next Step

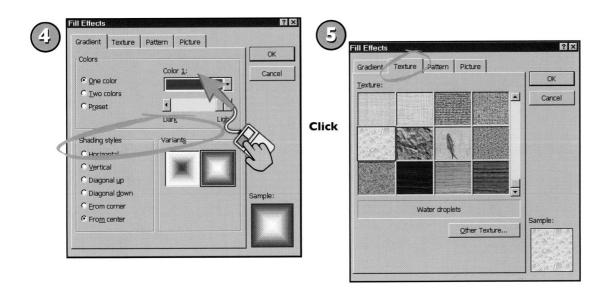

Click

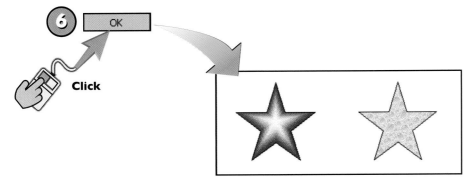

Click

④ Choose a color, and select one of the **Shading styles** and **Variants**.

⑤ Or, select the **Texture** tab in the Fill Effects dialog box, and click to select one of the textures. A description of the selected texture appears towards the bottom of the dialog box.

⑥ Click **OK** in the Fill Effects dialog box, and again in the Format AutoShapes dialog box. The formats are applied to the selected object.

✓ Copying Formats from One Object to Another

If you want to apply the same formatting to several objects, select the objects and format them all at once. If one object already has the formatting you want applied to other objects, select the object and click the **Format Painter** button (paint brush) on the **Standard** toolbar. Then click the object you want to format.

Task 10: Layering Slide Objects

Rearranging the Order of Slide Objects

Each object on a slide sits on an invisible layer. It's kind of like creating a slide by drawing each element on a separate sheet of tracing paper and stacking all the sheets. The first object on the slide is on the bottom layer. The most recently added object is on the top layer. You can reorder the layering of the slide objects by using the **Draw** button on the Drawing toolbar.

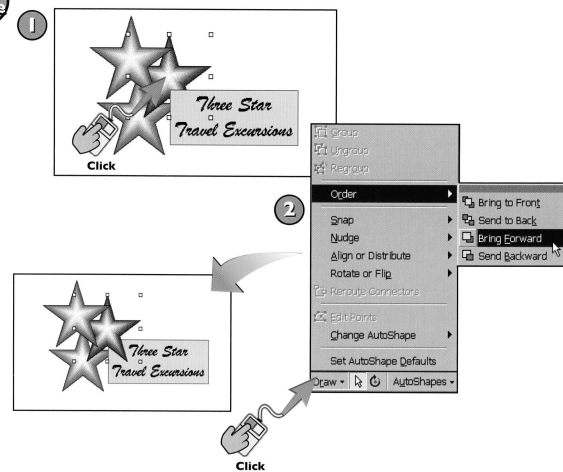

Start Here

Click

Click

① To change the layering of slide objects, select the object you want to reorder.

② To bring an object forward one layer, choose **Draw**, **Order**, **Bring Forward**. The object moves up one layer. (The selected star is now in front of the text.)

Next Step

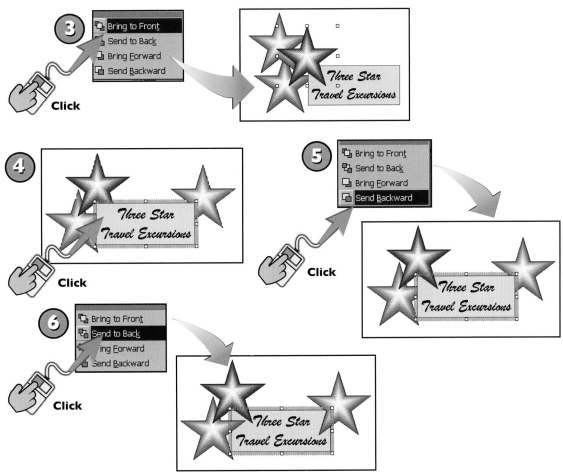

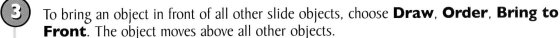

3 To bring an object in front of all other slide objects, choose **Draw**, **Order**, **Bring to Front**. The object moves above all other objects.

4 To move an object back one layer, start by selecting the object.

5 Choose **Draw**, **Order**, **Send Backward**. The object moves back one layer.

6 To place an object on the bottom layer, choose **Draw**, **Order**, **Send to Back**. The object moves behind all other objects.

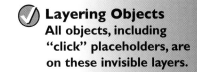

✓ **Layering Objects**
All objects, including "click" placeholders, are on these invisible layers.

End Task

Task 11: Grouping Slide Objects

Creating One Object from Several Objects

Most often, you will group objects to make them easier to move, copy, or resize. Grouping ensures the objects maintain their positions relative to each other.

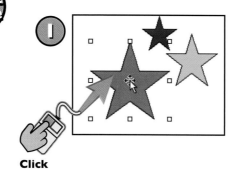

Click

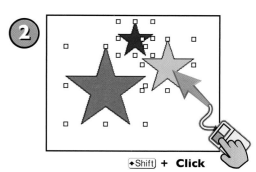

⬆Shift + Click

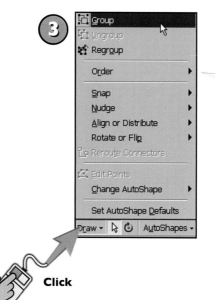

Click

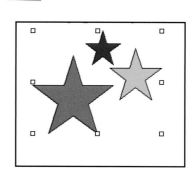

Start Here

✓ Ungrouping Objects
You can ungroup objects when you no longer need to maintain the group. Choose **Draw, Ungroup** from the Drawing toolbar.

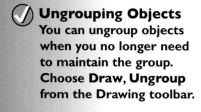

1 Click to select the first object.

2 Press **Shift** and click each additional object.

3 Choose **Draw**, **Group** from the Drawing toolbar. The selected objects now have one set of selection handles.

Next Step

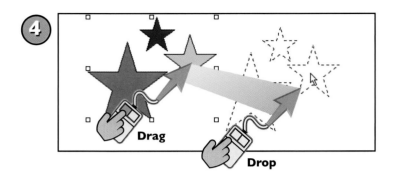

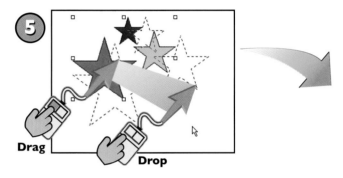

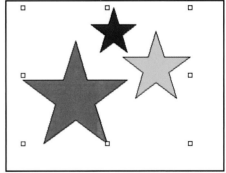

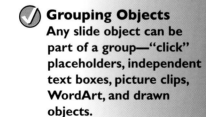

4 Now if you drag and drop the grouped objects, they move together and maintain their positions relative to each other. You can press **Ctrl** and drag to copy the grouped objects.

5 Drag from a corner selection handle to resize the grouped objects. The object sizes change in proportion to each other, without the need to resize each object separately.

Grouping Objects
Any slide object can be part of a group—"click" placeholders, independent text boxes, picture clips, WordArt, and drawn objects.

Working with Graphic Charts

With PowerPoint you can create a variety of graphic charts, including such common chart types as Column, Pie, and Line. You can also create a number of less common charts, such as Combination, Doughnut, and Bubble charts.

When you create or edit a chart in PowerPoint, you work in a separate program called Microsoft Graph. You enter the chart's data in a spreadsheet-like window called the Datasheet. Microsoft Graph has its own menu bar and toolbars.

Tasks

Task 1: Creating a Graphic Chart

Using the Chart Slide Layout

When you create a graphic chart in PowerPoint, you work in a separate program called Microsoft Graph. Within PowerPoint, the commands on the menu bar and the buttons on the toolbars become Microsoft Graph commands and buttons.

Start Here

① **Click**

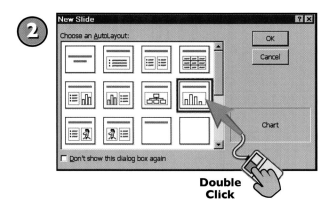

② **Double Click**

③ **Click to add title**

Double click to add chart

Double Click

✓ **Inserting a Chart**
To insert a chart into an existing slide, choose **Insert, Chart.**

① Click the **New Slide** button on the Standard toolbar.

② Double-click **Chart layout** in the New Slide dialog box. The new slide appears with the chart layout.

③ Double-click the chart placeholder to open Microsoft Graph and create the chart.

Next Step

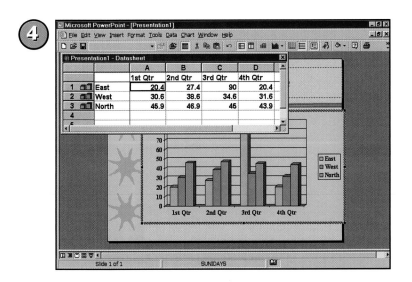

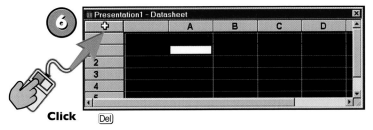

Click [Del]

4 A spreadsheet-like window—the Datasheet—appears, containing sample data. A chart graphing the sample data is displayed behind the Datasheet.

5 The Microsoft Graph menu bar and Standard toolbar include chart-specific options.

6 To clear the sample data in the Datasheet, click the gray box in the upper-left corner of the Datasheet and press **Delete**.

✓ Understanding the Chart Border
When you create or edit a chart, the chart displays a slash-mark border.

✓ Filling in the Datasheet
See Part 6, Task 2 for steps on entering your data in the Datasheet.

✓ Using Excel Data
See Part 6, Task 5 for steps on importing data from an Excel worksheet into the Microsoft Graph Datasheet.

End Task

Task 2: Entering Chart Data

Entering and Editing Data in the Datasheet

The Datasheet is made up of numbered rows and columns labeled with letters from the alphabet. The intersection of a row and a column is called a *cell*.

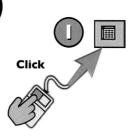

Start Here

Click

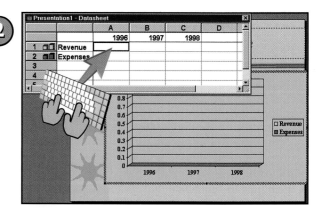

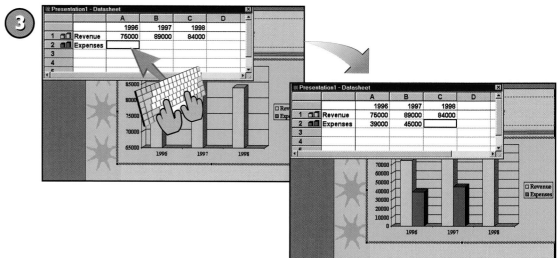

 Moving Around in the Datasheet

To move to another cell in the Datasheet, press **Enter** to move down or use the keyboard arrow keys to move in the direction you want.

1 If you don't see the Datasheet, click the **View Datasheet** button on the Standard toolbar.

2 Use the first row and column to type the headings, or labels, that describe the data you are going to chart. As you type the headings, the legend and frame for the chart appear.

3 As you type each row of data, Microsoft Graph plots a series of columns on the chart. To change the data, select the cell and type over the old data. To exit the Edit mode, click outside the Datasheet or chart placeholder.

End Task

Task 3: Editing a Chart

Start Here

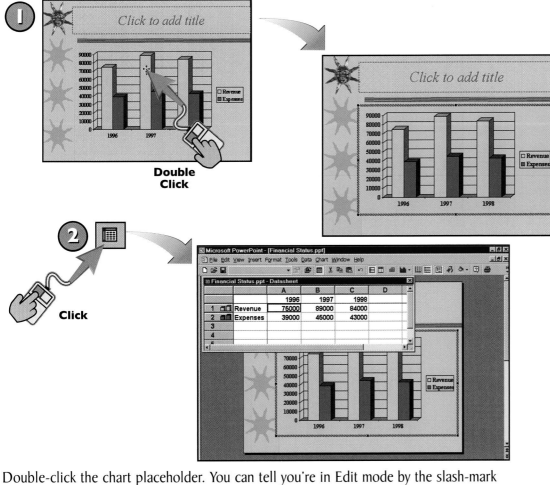

Double Click

Click

1 Double-click the chart placeholder. You can tell you're in Edit mode by the slash-mark border around the chart placeholder.

2 To display the Datasheet, click the **View Datasheet** button on the Standard toolbar. To change the data, select the cell and type over the old data. To add data, click in a blank cell and type.

Modifying an Existing Chart

Before you can change the chart data or chart type, you must be in the chart Edit mode.

✅ **Exiting the Edit Mode**
If you click outside the Datasheet or chart placeholder, you will exit the Edit mode.

✅ **Selecting a Chart Type**
See Part 6, Task 7 to learn how to change the chart type.

End Task

Adding and Removing Rows or Columns in Your Datasheet

Make room for new data by inserting extra rows or columns in the Datasheet. When you no longer need a row or column in the Datasheet, delete it.

Task 4: Inserting and Deleting Datasheet Rows and Columns

 Start Here

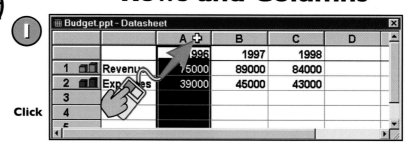

Click

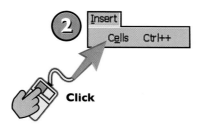

Click

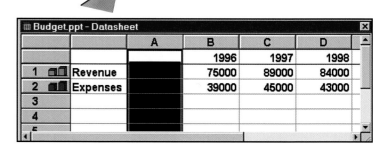

✓ **Selecting Multiple Rows or Columns**
To select more than one row or column, drag the mouse pointer across the gray area displaying the row or column labels.

① Click the row or column where you want to insert the new row or column. When you insert new rows, existing rows move down. When you insert new columns, existing columns move right.

② Choose **Insert**, **Cells**. PowerPoint inserts the new row or column.

 Next Step

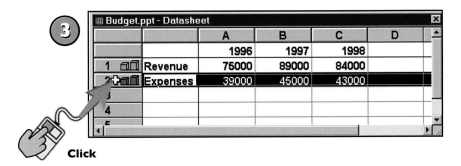

Click

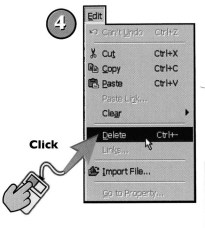

Click

3 Click the label of the row or column you want to delete.

4 Choose **Edit**, **Delete**. PowerPoint deletes the selected row or column. The remaining rows and columns adjust.

✅ **Accidentally Deleting a Row or Column**
If you delete a row or column accidentally, choose **Edit, Undo**.

End Task

Task 5: Importing Data from Excel into the Datasheet

Using Excel Data to Create a PowerPoint Chart

If the data you want to use for a PowerPoint chart already exists in an Excel worksheet, you can save time by copying the data from Excel instead of retyping it.

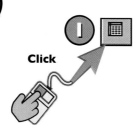

Click

Click

Click

✅ **Clearing the Datasheet**
Unless you are adding Excel data to an existing PowerPoint chart, you should clear all data from the Datasheet. See Part 6, Task 1 for the steps to clear the data.

① Make sure you are in the chart Edit mode. If the Datasheet is not displayed, click the **View Datasheet** button on the Standard toolbar.

② Select the cell in which you want the first piece of Excel data to appear—usually, it's the cell that intersects the header row and column.

③ Open or switch to Excel.

④ Open the Excel file containing the data you want to bring into PowerPoint.

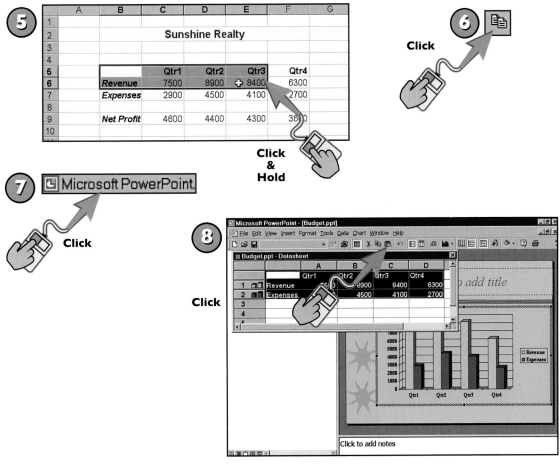

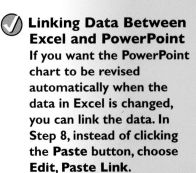

5 Drag to select the data in Excel that you want to copy into the PowerPoint Datasheet.

6 Click the **Copy** button on the Standard toolbar.

7 Switch back to PowerPoint by clicking the **Microsoft PowerPoint** button on the taskbar.

8 Click the **Paste** button to insert the data from Excel.

✅ **Linking Data Between Excel and PowerPoint**
If you want the PowerPoint chart to be revised automatically when the data in Excel is changed, you can link the data. In Step 8, instead of clicking the **Paste** button, choose **Edit, Paste Link.**

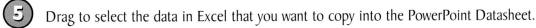

Plotting the Data by Rows or Columns

Depending on the information you are trying to convey to your audience, you might prefer to switch the way the data is plotted in the chart.

Task 6: Switching the Plot of the Chart Data

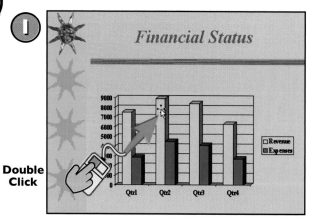

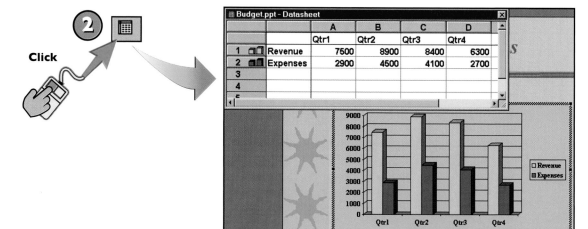

✓ Understanding Chart Terminology

The data being plotted is called the *data series*. The groups of data along the x-axis are called the *data categories*. In the example in this task, the data series are Revenue and Expenses. The data categories are the quarters.

1 Position the mouse pointer over the chart. The pointer changes to a four-headed arrow. Double-click the chart to get into the Edit mode.

2 Click the **View Datasheet** button on the Standard toolbar to display the Datasheet. Notice each row number also has a colored chart symbol, and the data in each row is plotted in the chart. The row headings appear in the legend; the column headings appear on the x-axis.

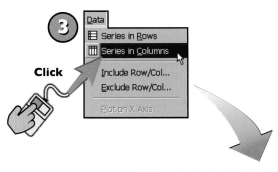

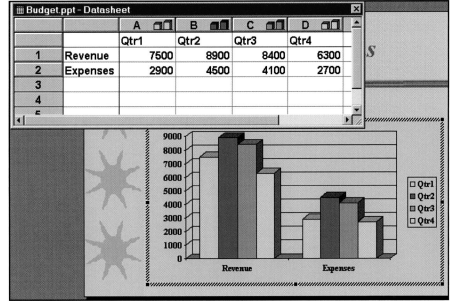

✔ **Seeing the Series Being Changed**
You do not have to display the Datasheet to change the data the chart plots, but doing so makes it easier to identify the data series.

✔ **Using Toolbar Buttons to Switch the Plot**
Notice the icons displayed in Step 3 next to the Series in Rows and the Series in Columns commands. Look for buttons containing these icons on the Standard toolbar. Those buttons do the same thing as these two menu commands.

3 To plot the column data in the chart, choose **Data**, **Series in Columns**. Now the data in each column is plotted, and each column letter has a colored chart symbol. The column headings appear in the legend; the row headings appear on the x-axis.

Task 7: Selecting a Chart Type

Changing the Chart Type

You can choose from 14 charts in PowerPoint, each with its own uses. The default chart type is a three-dimensional column chart. Most types have two-dimensional and three-dimensional variations.

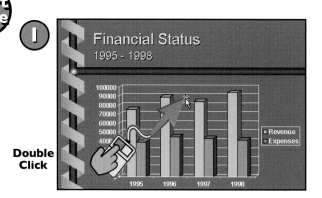

Double Click

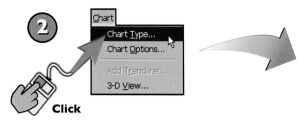

Click

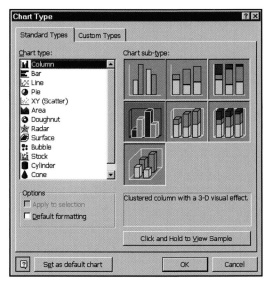

 **Using Built-in Custom Chart Types**

Several unique chart types are available on the Custom Types tab in the Chart Type dialog box, including charts that combine columns and lines.

1 Position the mouse pointer in the middle of the chart. The pointer changes to a four-headed arrow. Double-click the chart to get into the Edit mode.

2 Choose **Chart**, **Chart Type**. The Chart Type dialog box appears with the active chart type highlighted.

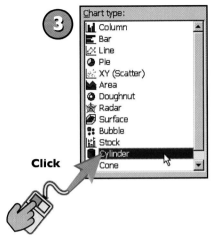

Click

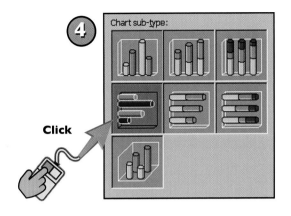

Click

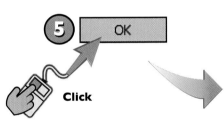

OK

Click

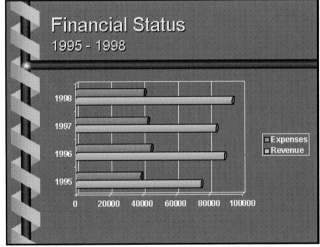

Financial Status
1995 - 1998

Expenses
Revenue

(3) In the **Chart type** list, scroll to see the list of chart types available in PowerPoint. Then select the type of chart you want.

(4) The **Chart sub-type** list displays all the variations of the chart type you have selected. Click to select a sub-type.

(5) Choose **OK** to change the chart type.

Choosing the Right Chart Type
Line charts are a good choice when you have more than four or five data series or data categories. Pie charts plot only one data series—for example, revenue for each year (but no expenses) or revenue and expenses for 1998 (but not the other years). Cylinder, Cone, and Pyramid charts are attractive variations of column and bar charts.

Task 8: Changing Chart Options

Adjusting the Chart Features

Using the Chart Options dialog box, you can select and customize the features that appear on a chart. These features include chart titles, gridlines, legends, data labels, and data tables. You must be in Edit mode to access the Chart Options dialog box; double-click the chart to switch to Edit mode.

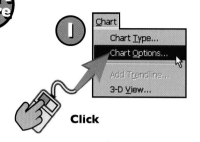

Click

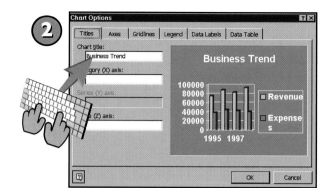

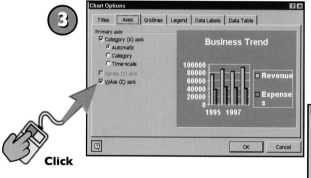

Click

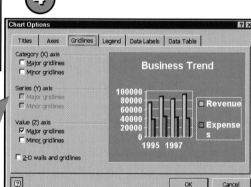

Click

Click

(1) Choose **Chart**, **Chart Options** to display the Chart Options dialog box.

(2) On the **Titles** tab, you can type a title for the chart or for the axes.

(3) The **Axes** tab has options for showing the chart axes. Generally, the Value and Category axes should be displayed. Click to select or deselect options on this tab.

(4) The **Gridlines** tab includes options for displaying chart gridlines. Most charts show gridlines for the major value axis. Click to select or deselect options.

Next
Step

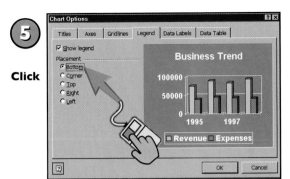

Click

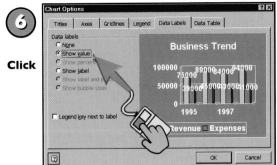

Click

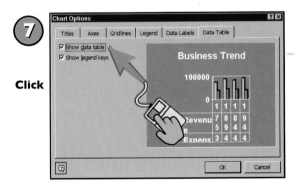

Click

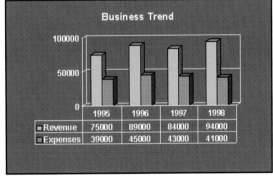

✅ **Chart Formatting Options**
See Part 6, Task 9 for steps on formatting the parts of the chart, including the color of the data series, the scale of the axes, and the legend.

✅ **Chart Preview Is Just a Sample**
The preview in the Chart Options dialog box attempts to show as much data as possible, given its limited space. Click **OK** to see the full chart.

(5) On the **Legend** tab, choose a location for the legend. The most common placements are **Right** and **Bottom**.

(6) On the **Data Labels** tab, click **Show value** to display the plotted number next to each data series.

(7) On the **Data Table** tab, click **Show data table** to display a table below your chart, similar to the Datasheet. Use a data table instead of data labels; you won't need a separate legend because the table includes a legend. Click **OK** to change the chart.

End Task

Task 9: Formatting Chart Components

Changing the Appearance of the Chart

Options in the Format dialog box let you change your chart's appearance. For example, you can change the color for the data series, unclutter the scale of the Value axis, and add a drop shadow and background color to the legend. When you right-click a part of the chart you want to change, the shortcut menu appears; use it to access the Format dialog box.

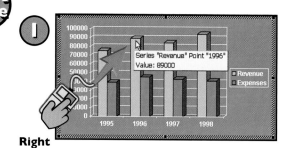

Start Here!

①

Right Click

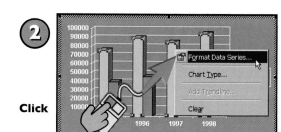

②

Click

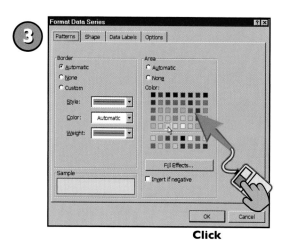

③

Click

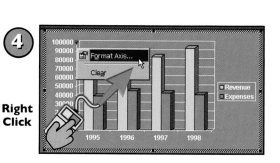

④

Right Click

① Right-click the data series.

② Choose **Format Data Series** from the shortcut menu. The Format Data Series dialog box opens.

③ Use the options on the **Patterns** tab to adjust the color of the series. Choose **OK** to see the changes on the chart.

④ To format an axis, right-click the axis and choose **Format Axis** from the shortcut menu. The Format Axis dialog box opens.

Next Step

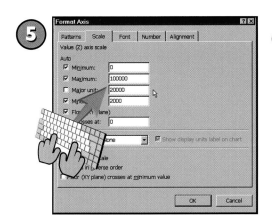

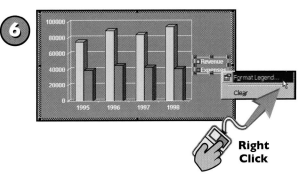

Right Click

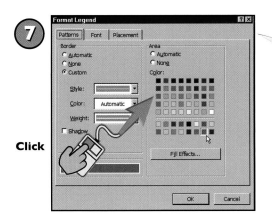

Click

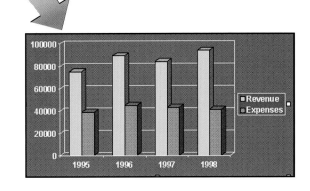

✅ **Identifying the Parts of a Chart**
Whenever you rest the mouse pointer over a part of the chart, a ScreenTip identifies the part, as shown in Step 1.

✅ **Understanding the Value Axis**
The Value Axis shows a range of numbers corresponding to the numbers the data series plots. The range is usually from zero to a number slightly higher than the largest number plotted.

5 Use the options on the **Scale** tab to adjust the scale of the Value axes. Type the values and click **OK** to see the changes on the chart.

6 Right-click anywhere on the legend and choose **Format Legend** from the shortcut menu. The Format Legend dialog box opens.

7 Use the options on the **Patterns** tab to format the legend's border and background color. Click **OK** to see the changes on the chart.

End Task

Working with Organization Charts

PowerPoint includes a program specifically designed for creating organization charts. The program—called Microsoft Organization Chart—appears in its own window, separate from PowerPoint.

The information about each person or position in an organization chart is placed in a box, which you can format by changing colors and fonts or by adding drop shadows. You can even make the boxes display vertically instead of the traditional horizontal arrangement seen in most organization charts.

Tasks

Task 1: Creating an Organization Chart

Using the Organization Chart Slide Layout

When you create an organization chart in PowerPoint, you work in a separate program called Microsoft Organization Chart. This program appears in a separate window.

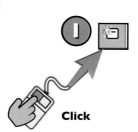

Start Here

Click

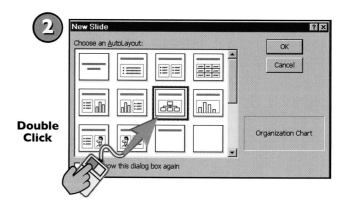

Double Click

Double Click

✓ **Inserting an Organization Chart**
To insert a chart into an existing slide, choose **Insert, Picture, Organization Chart.**

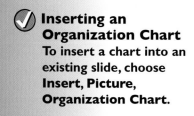

① Select the **New Slide** button on the Standard toolbar.

② Double-click the **Organization Chart** layout in the New Slide dialog box.

③ The new slide appears with the chart layout. Double-click the organization chart placeholder to create the chart.

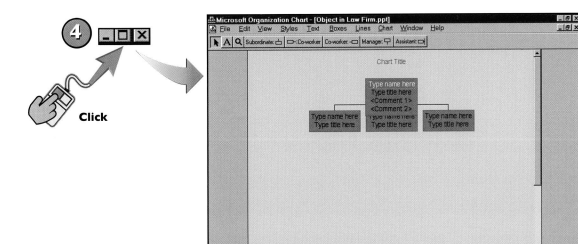

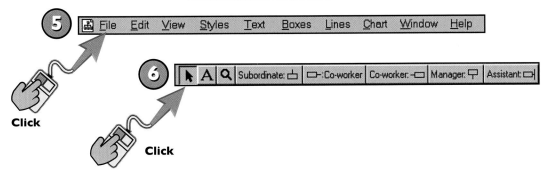

Click

④ The Microsoft Organization Chart program appears in a separate window with a new organization chart started. Click the **Maximize** button to make the window full screen.

⑤ The Organization Chart program has its own menu bar containing commands. Click the commands to create and modify organization charts.

⑥ The Organization Chart toolbar is primarily used to add people to your organization chart.

✓ **Filling in the Organization Chart**
See Part 7, Task 2 for steps on entering names and titles in the Organization Chart boxes.

✓ **Adding More Positions to an Organization Chart**
See Part 7, Task 3 for steps on adding more people to your Organization Chart.

Start Building Your Organization Chart

An organization chart is made up of a series of boxes that hold information about the people or positions in your organization. Each box can contain the name and pertinent information for one person or position. The box can hold up to four lines of text.

Task 2: Entering Names and Titles into an Organization Chart

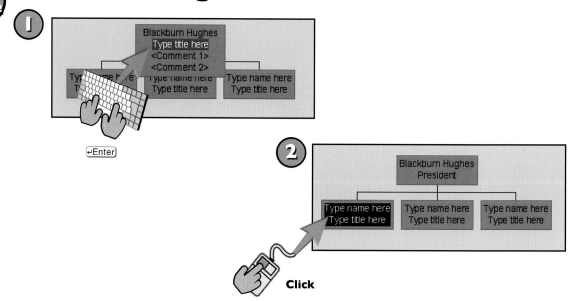

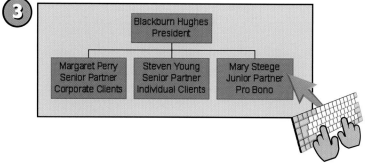

Click

(✓) **Adding More Positions to the Organization Chart**
See Part 7, Task 3 for the steps to add more people to your chart.

(1) When you create an Organization Chart, the first box is active. Type the first line; then press **Enter** to activate the next line. Type the remaining text, pressing **Enter** for each new line.

(2) Click the next box in which you want to enter data, and type the information.

(3) Complete the information in each box you want to be part of your organization chart.

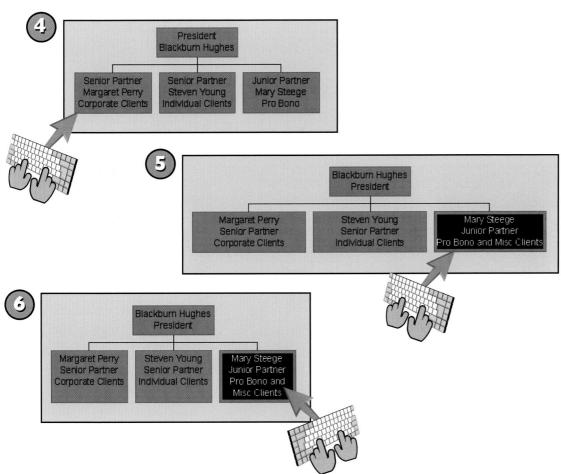

✓ **Moving People in an Organization Chart**
See Part 7, Task 4 for the steps to move a person from one part of the Organization Chart to another.

✓ **Formatting Organization Chart Text and Boxes**
See Part 7, Task 6 for steps on formatting the text and style of the boxes.

4 The boxes suggest entering the name in the first line; however, you can type the information in any order you wish. Here, the name and title appear below the category of work.

5 The longest line in a box dictates the horizontal width of all boxes on the same level.

6 The box containing the most lines of information dictates the vertical height of all boxes on the same level.

Inserting and Deleting Boxes in the Organization Chart

To add people to the organization chart, use the box buttons on the toolbar. You can add positions below (subordinates), next to (coworkers), and above (managers) other positions in the organization chart. You can even add boxes for assistants.

Task 3: Adding and Deleting People in an Organization Chart

Double Click

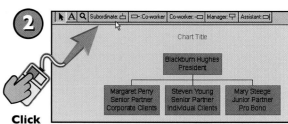

Click

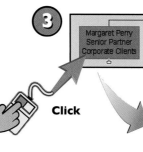

Click

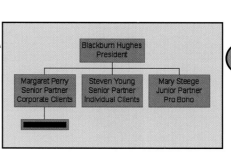

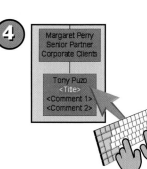

✅ **Adding Multiple Positions at Once**

To add more than one box at a time, use multiple clicks; the number of clicks determines the number of boxes added.

① Double-click the chart to open the Organization Chart program.

② To add a person below someone on the chart, click once on the **Subordinate** button.

③ Position the mouse pointer in the box where you want to add the new person. Click the box to add the person; PowerPoint adds the new box to the chart.

④ Type the information in the new box.

Next Step

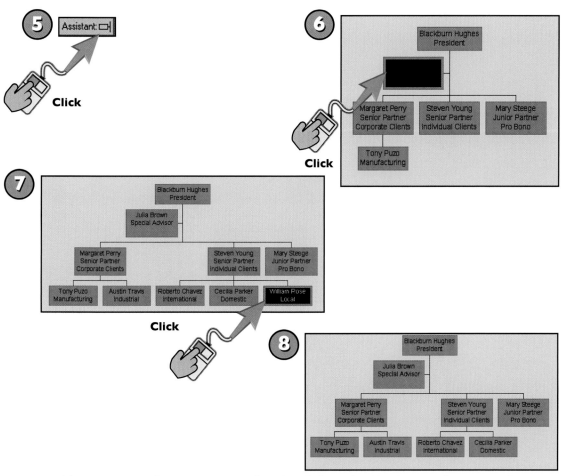

Selecting Multiple Boxes
To select more than one box, click the first box. Then press **Shift** and click the other boxes you want to select.

WARNING
When you delete a manager, PowerPoint deletes all of that manager's subordinates, too. To keep the subordinates, move them under someone else before deleting the manager. See Part 7, Task 4 to learn how to move people in your organization chart.

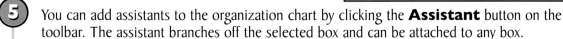

(5) You can add assistants to the organization chart by clicking the **Assistant** button on the toolbar. The assistant branches off the selected box and can be attached to any box.

(6) Click the person to whom the assistant will be assigned. The assistant box appears below and to the left of the selected box; boxes can have more than one assistant.

(7) To remove a box, first click it.

(8) Then press the **Delete** key. The organization chart layout automatically adjusts.

End Task

Task 4: Moving People in an Organization Chart

Changing the Order of the Boxes in the Organization Chart

You can move people to different positions in the organization chart by dragging their box next to a coworker or manager.

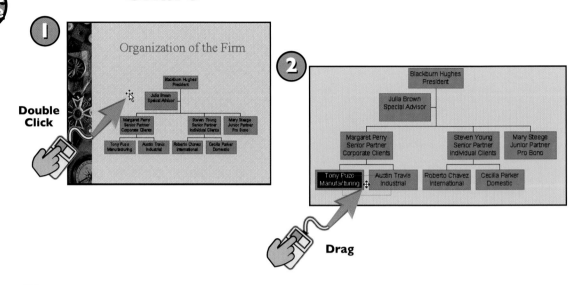

Start Here

Double Click

Drag

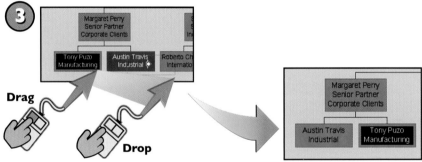

Drag

Drop

WARNING

Do not select the box you are going to move. Hold down the mouse pointer on the box and immediately drag the mouse to move it. Selecting a box first makes it difficult to move.

1 Double-click the chart to open the Organization Chart program.

2 To move a box, position the mouse pointer over the box. Hold down the mouse button and drag the mouse. The mouse pointer changes to a four-headed arrow.

3 The mouse pointer changes to a pointing arrow to indicate the placement of the box you are dragging in relation to the box your mouse pointer is resting on. In this example, Tony Puzo will be placed to the right of Austin Travis.

Next Step

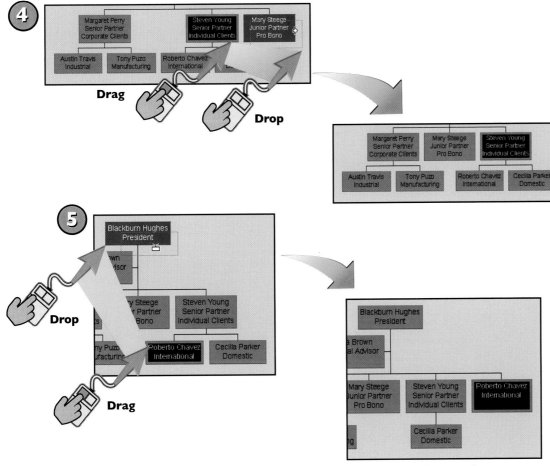

Drag

Drop

Drop

Drag

④ To move a manager and his subordinates, drag and drop the manager to his new location.

⑤ To move a person up or down levels in the chart, drag and drop his box. To make one person subordinate to another person, drag their box to the manager's box (as shown here). The mouse symbol indicates the relationship between the box you are dragging and the destination box.

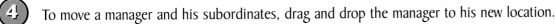

✓ **Levels Versus Branches**
Each row of boxes is known as a *level*. A manager and subordinates together are called a *branch*.

✓ **Formatting Organization Chart Boxes**
See Part 7, Task 6 for steps to format the boxes in the organization chart.

Working with the Box Styles

The **Organization Chart** program includes several flexible box layout styles you can use. Styles can display the boxes vertically, horizontally, or without borders. Before you can alter the box styles, you must first select the boxes you want to change.

Task 5: Formatting the Box Layout in an Organization Chart

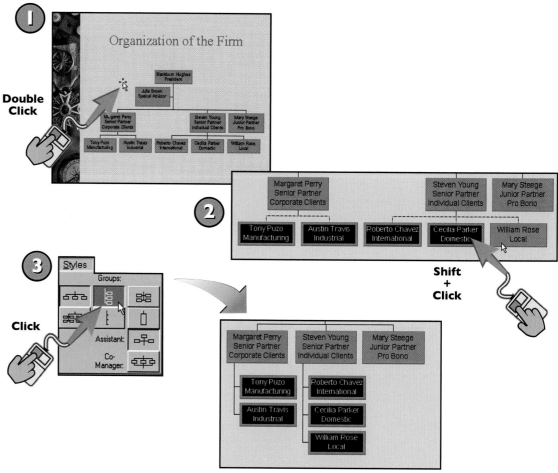

Double Click

Shift + Click

Click

✓ **Selecting All Boxes on a Specific Level**
Each row of boxes in the organization chart is considered a level. Use the **Edit, Select Levels** command to select boxes based on level.

① Double-click the chart to open the Organization Chart program.

② Click to select a box. To select additional boxes, press **Shift** and click the other boxes you want to select.

③ Then click the **Styles** menu and click a box style layout. This style displays the boxes in one vertical column.

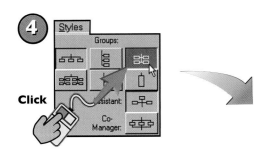

Click

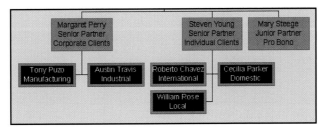

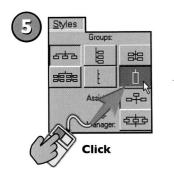

Click

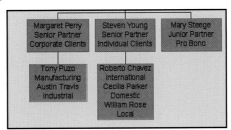

④ To display the boxes in two columns, click the **Styles** menu and select the top right layout. This allows for more people per manager to be visible.

⑤ To pool everyone in each branch into a single box, click the **Styles** menu and select the layout on the far right, second row. This style is best when only one line of information— either a name or a title—is used for each person.

✓ **Selecting Groups or Branches**
Choose **Edit, Select** to see a list of selection options. To use the Group or Branch option, you must first select a box. All the other options do not require you to select anything first.

✓ **Branches Versus Groups**
A branch is the set of boxes below (subordinate to) the active box. A *group* is the set of boxes on the same level as the active box.

✓ **Changing Text Size**
See Part 7, Task 6 for steps to reduce the font size of the text.

Changing the Text and Box Attributes

You can alter the text and box appearance for one box or a group of boxes. You can even apply formatting to individual lines in a box. The box attributes include color, drop shadows, and border styles.

Task 6: Formatting Text and Boxes in an Organization Chart

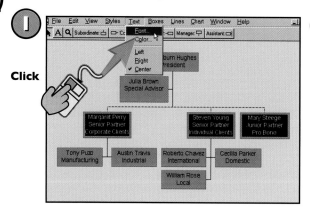

Click

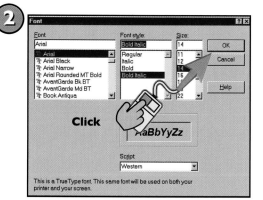

Click

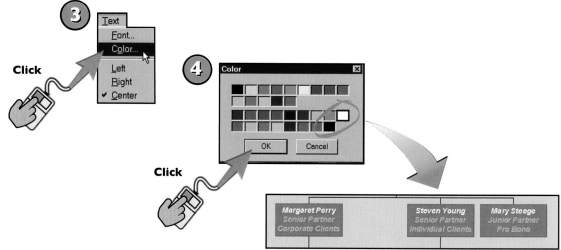

Click

Click

✓ Selecting Boxes

The **Edit, Select** command provides several useful options for selecting organization chart components. Choose **All Non-Managers**, for example, to select every person who does not have subordinates.

1. Select the boxes containing the text you want to format. To format a single line of text, drag the mouse pointer across the text to highlight the text. Then choose **Text**, **Font** from the menu bar.

2. In the Font dialog box, choose the font, the style, and the size. Click **OK** to apply the changes to the text.

3. To change the text's color, choose **Text**, **Color** from the menu bar.

4. In the Color dialog box, click the color you want and choose **OK**.

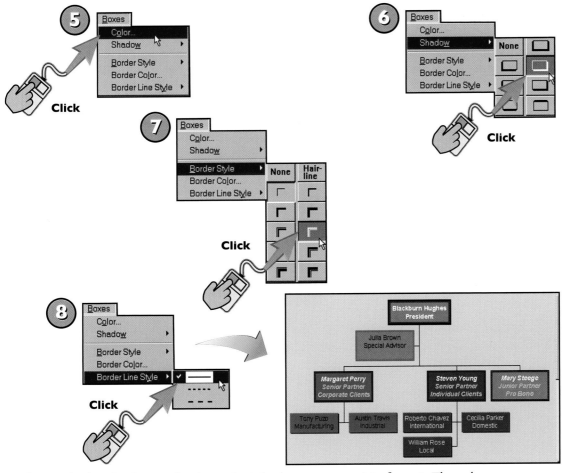

⑤ To change the box background color, select the boxes you want to format. Then choose **Boxes**, **Color** and select a color.

⑥ To apply a drop shadow to a box, choose **Boxes**, **Shadow** and select the shadow position.

⑦ To change the box border appearance, choose **Boxes**, **Border Style** and select a style.

⑧ To change the type of line used on the box's border, choose **Boxes**, **Border Line Style** and select a style.

✅ **Selecting Specific Text in a Box**
When you want to change only one line of text in a box, select it by dragging the mouse pointer (a thin capital "I") across the text.

✅ **Use Contrasting Colors**
When selecting a box background color, make sure it contrasts with the text color. White (or light) text does not show up well on a yellow background. Black (or dark) text does not show up well on a blue background.

End Task

Task 7: Updating Your Presentation with the Organization Chart

Exiting the Organization Chart Program

Because you create organization charts in a separate program, you must exit the program to see the organization chart in your PowerPoint presentation.

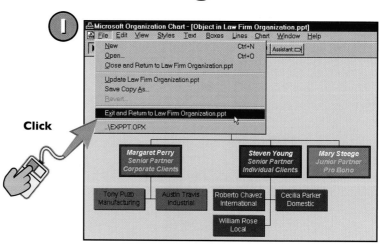

Click

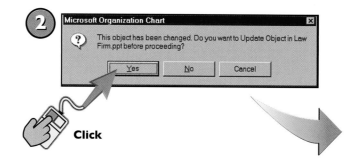

Click

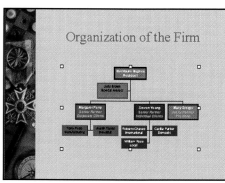

Organization of the Firm

✓ **Saving Organization Charts as Separate Files**

The File menu contains options to save (and subsequently open) organization charts you intend to use in several presentations, thus saving you the trouble of re-creating them.

① Choose **File**, **Exit and Return** to close the Organization Chart program and update your presentation with the changes made to the chart.

② Click **Yes** in the update dialog box. The chart displays in the presentation slide.

Next Step

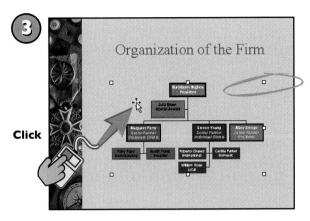

Click

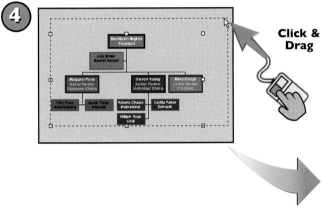

Click & Drag

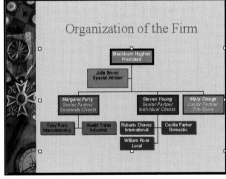

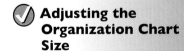

③ Sometimes the organization chart is displayed smaller than you expect. Start by selecting the chart; a set of selection handles appears around the chart.

④ Then position the mouse pointer on a corner selection handle and drag to enlarge the chart. Always use a corner selection handle to avoid distorting the slide.

✅ **Adjusting the Organization Chart Size**
You may be able to enlarge an organization chart by reapplying the slide layout. Choose **Format, Slide Layout** and click the **Reapply** button.

Working with Tables

You can add a table to a slide in PowerPoint. Tables are especially useful for displaying lists of data or comparing two or more sets of data. A list of product names and prices or a comparison of sales from this year and last year can be more clearly displayed in a table, for example, than in paragraphs of text.

After you create a table, you can use the Tables and Borders toolbar to make virtually any changes or formatting you want to the table.

If you are familiar with creating and modifying tables in Microsoft Word, you will find that most of the features and capabilities are identical in PowerPoint.

Tasks

Task 1: Creating a Table

Using the Table Slide Layout

When you create a table in PowerPoint, you are asked how many rows and columns you want for the table. You can add additional rows and columns as needed.

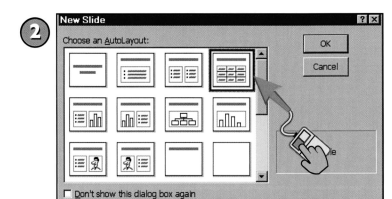

Click

Double Click

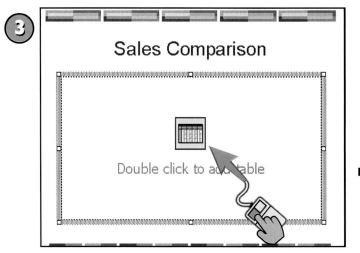

Sales Comparison

Double click to add table

Double Click

(✓) **Insering a Table**
To insert a table into an existing slide, choose Insert, Table.

① Click the **New Slide** button on the Standard toolbar.

② In the New Slide dialog box, double-click the **Table layout**.

③ The new slide appears with the Table layout. Double-click the table placeholder to create the table.

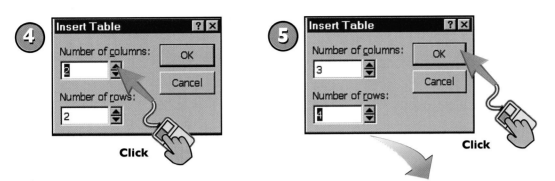

Click

Click

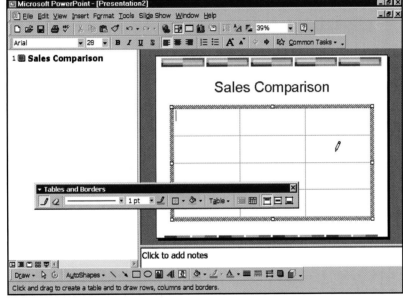

④ The Insert Table dialog box appears. Use the spinner buttons (the arrow buttons at the end of the text boxes) to select the number of rows and columns you need.

⑤ After you select the number of rows and columns, click **OK**. The table appears in the slide, ready for you to enter the data.

✅ **Filling in the Table**
See Part 8, Task 2 for steps on entering or editing table data.

✅ **Adding More Rows and Columns**
See Part 8, Task 5 for steps on inserting rows and columns.

✅ **Merging and Splitting Cells**
See Part 8, Task 7 for steps on combining and breaking apart cells in a table.

Inserting and Changing Table Data

A table is made up of rows and columns. The intersection of a row and column is a cell. A flashing cursor indicates the active cell, or location, in a table. You enter and modify text in a table the same as you do in any text object.

Task 2: Entering and Editing Text in a Table

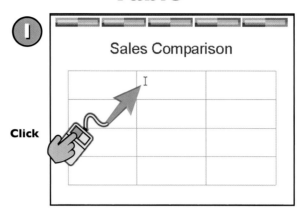

Start Here

Click

Sales Comparison

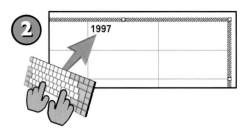

1997

②

③

1997

Tab⇥

	1997	1998
Walking Shoes	$64,000	$78,000
Sandals	$29,000	$31,000
Hiking Boots	$15,000	$33,000

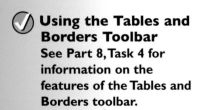

✓ **Using the Tables and Borders Toolbar**
See Part 8, Task 4 for information on the features of the Tables and Borders toolbar.

① Click in the cell to which you want to add text; the flashing cursor appears in the cell.

② Type the text.

③ Press the **Tab** key to move to the next cell; continue until you've typed in all the text.

Next Step

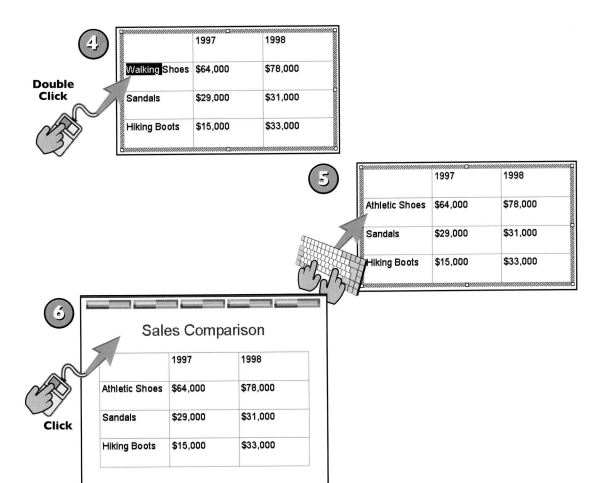

4 To edit text in a table, double-click to select a word or triple-click to select all the words in that cell.

5 As you type, the new data replaces the highlighted text.

6 Click outside the table when you have finished entering or editing the text.

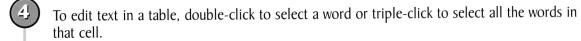

✅ **Changing Row or Column Size**
See Part 8, Task 3 for steps to adjust the row height or column width.

✅ **Formatting the Table**
See Part 8, Task 8 to change the text alignment.

See Part 8, Task 9 to learn how to format the borders and gridlines in a table.

Adjusting Row Height and Column Width

Before you can adjust the size of a row or column, you must first get into the edit mode by clicking in the table. Then use the mouse to drag the row and column borders to change the row height and column width.

Task 3: Changing Row and Column Size

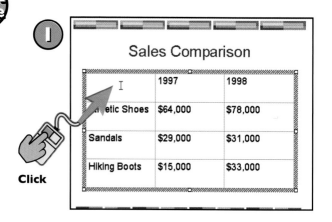

Click

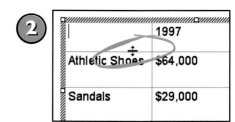

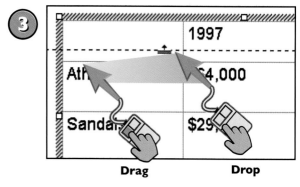

Drag   Drop

✓ **Adding More Rows and Columns**
See Part 8, Task 5 for steps on inserting rows and columns.

① Click anywhere inside the table to edit the table. The slash mark border indicates you're in edit mode.

② To change a row's height, position the mouse pointer on the row border you want to adjust. The mouse changes to a parallel line with arrows pointing up and down.

③ Drag the border to the new position. A dotted line appears to guide you while you adjust the border.

④ When you release the mouse, the adjustment is made.

5

	1997	1998
Athletic Shoes	$64,000	$78,000
Sandals	$29,000	$31,000
Hiking Boots	$15,000	$33,000

6

	1997	1998
Athletic Shoes	$64,000	$78,000
Sandals	,000	$31,000

Drop

Drag

7

	1997	1998
Athletic Shoes	$64,000	$78,000
Sandals	$29,000	$31,000

5 To change the width of a column, position the mouse pointer on the column border you want to adjust. The mouse changes to a parallel line with arrows pointing left and right.

6 Drag the border to the new position. A dotted line appears to guide you while you adjust the border.

7 When you release the mouse, the adjustment is made.

Merging and Splitting Cells
See Part 8, Task 7 for steps on combining and breaking apart cells in a table.

End Task

Taking Advantage of the Tables and Borders Toolbar

Use the Tables and Borders toolbar to format and customize your table. When you create a table in PowerPoint, the toolbar automatically appears.

Task 4: Working with the Tables and Borders Toolbar

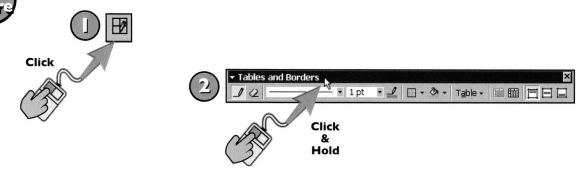

Click

Click & Hold

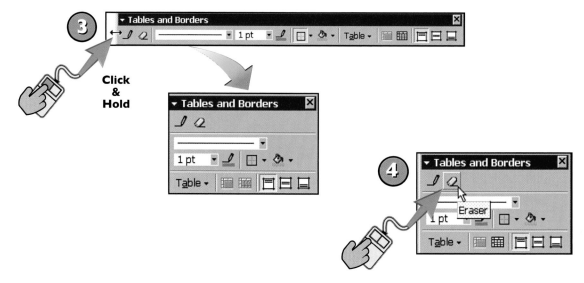

Click & Hold

✓ **Toolbar Sole Source for Options**
Most of the options on the Tables and Borders toolbar are not available through the PowerPoint menus.

① When you create or edit a table, the Tables and Borders toolbar appears. If you close or hide the toolbar, click the **Tables and Borders** button (on the Standard toolbar) to redisplay it.

② You can move the toolbar by dragging its title bar to a new position.

③ You can resize the toolbar by dragging the toolbar border.

④ You can identify each button on the Tables and Borders toolbar by resting the mouse pointer on the button. A ScreenTip appears and explains the purpose of the button.

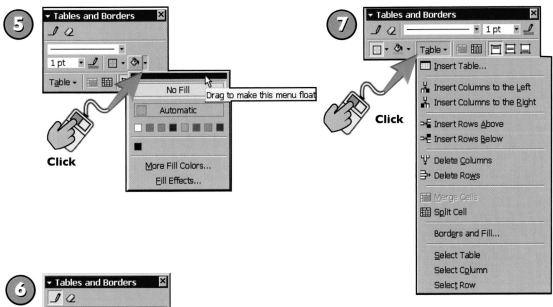

Click

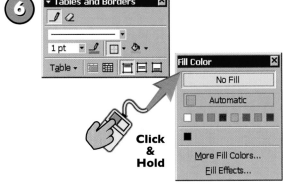

Click
&
Hold

5 Some of the drop-down menus have pull-off palettes. Hover the mouse over the bar at the top of the menu to make the **Drag to make this menu float** ToolTip appear.

6 Drag the dark band at the top end of the drop-down menu to keep the palette on the screen, like a mini-toolbar.

7 Click the **Table** drop-down menu on the toolbar to see a list of useful commands for inserting and deleting rows and columns, as well as splitting and merging cells.

✔ **Adding More Rows and Columns**
See Part 8, Task 5 for steps on inserting rows and columns.

✔ **Formatting the Table**
See Part 8, Task 8 to change the text alignment.

See Part 8, Task 9 to learn how to format the borders and gridlines in a table.

End
Task

Task 5: Inserting Rows and Columns

Adding Rows and Columns to a Table

You must be in **Edit** mode before you can insert new rows or columns in the table. Use the **Table** menu on the **Tables and Borders** toolbar to insert rows and columns.

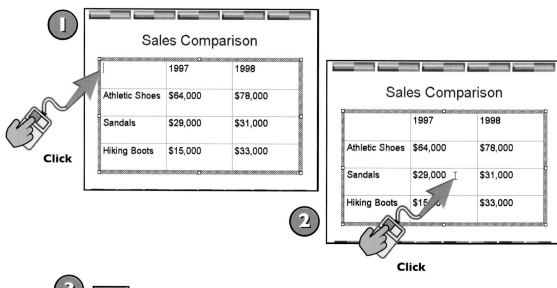

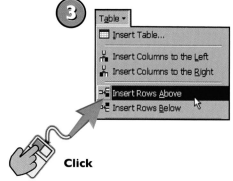

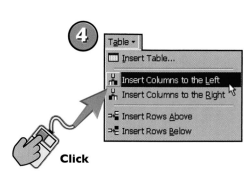

(✓) **Inserting One Row or Column**
PowerPoint looks for the active row or column to determine where it should insert a new row or column. The flashing cursor indicates the active row or column.

1. Click anywhere inside the table to edit it. The slash mark border indicates you're in Edit mode.

2. Click in a cell in the row or column where you want the new row or column to appear.

3. To insert a row, choose **Table**, **Insert Rows Above** or **Insert Rows Below** from the Tables and Borders toolbar.

4. To insert a column, choose **Table**, **Insert Columns to the Left** or **Insert Columns to the Right** from the Tables and Borders toolbar.

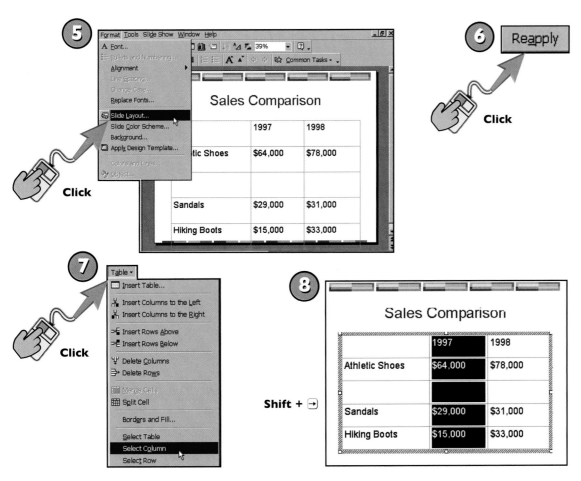

5 When you insert rows or columns, the table layout becomes distorted. With the table selected, choose **Format**, **Slide Layout**.

6 In the Slide Layout dialog box, choose **Reapply**. The rows or columns adjust automatically.

7 To select an entire row or column, choose **Table**, **Select Column** or **Select Row** from the Tables and Borders toolbar. All the cells in the row or column become highlighted.

8 Then, to highlight multiple rows or columns, press **Shift** and the keyboard arrow key that points in the direction you want to select.

✓ Adding Multiple Rows or Columns
When you want to insert multiple rows or columns at one time, you must first select them (see Steps 7 and 8). Then, choose the **Insert** option on the **Table** drop-down menu on the **Tables and Borders** toolbar.

Task 6: Deleting Rows and Columns

Removing Rows or Columns in a Table

You must be in Edit mode before you can delete rows or columns in the table. Use the **Table** menu on the **Tables and Borders** toolbar to delete rows and columns.

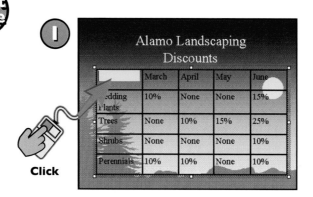

Click

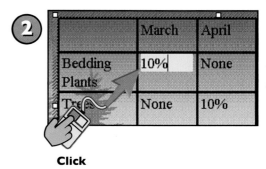

Click

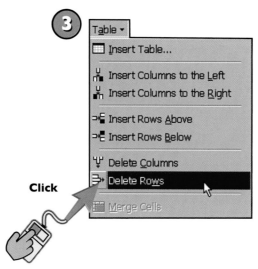

Click

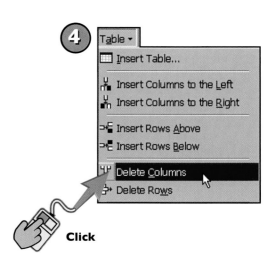

Click

✓ **PowerPoint Deletes the Active Row or Column**

PowerPoint looks for the active row or column to determine where it should delete a row or column. The flashing cursor indicates the active row or column.

1 Click anywhere inside the table to edit the table. The slash mark border indicates you're in edit mode.

2 Click in a cell in the row or column that you want to delete.

3 To delete a row, choose **Table**, **Delete Rows** from the Tables and Borders toolbar.

4 To delete a column, choose **Table**, **Delete Columns** from the Tables and Borders toolbar.

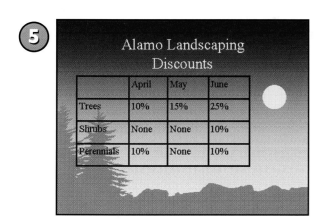

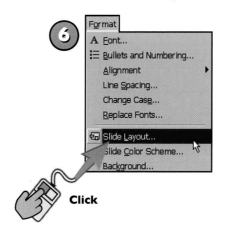

Click

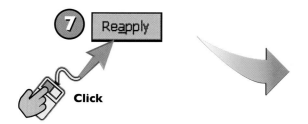

Click

✓ Table Layout Adjusts
When you delete a row or column, the remaining columns move to the left. The remaining rows move up.

✓ Using the Eraser
You can use the Eraser button on theables and Borders toolbar to remove row and column gridlines. Click the Eraser button and click the gridline you want to delete.

5 When you delete rows or columns, the table layout automatically shrinks.

6 To enlarge the table to fill the available space on the slide, choose **Format**, **Slide Layout**.

7 In the Slide Layout dialog box, choose **Reapply**. The table layout fills the appropriate area on the slide.

Task 7: Merging and Splitting Cells in a Table

Combining and Dividing Cells

One way to customize a table is to merge or split cells. Several cells can be combined into one cell, for example, to hold a table heading. A single cell can be split in two, providing an additional area to enter data.

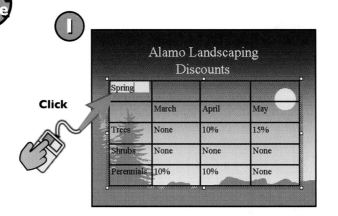

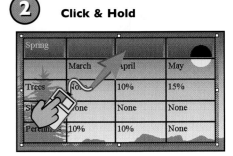

Click & Hold

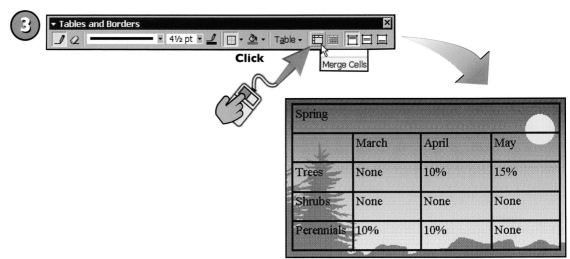

Click

Merge Cells

(✓) **Made a Mistake?**
If you accidentally merge or split the wrong cells, choose **Edit, Undo** to restore the cells.

① Click anywhere inside the table to edit the table. The slash mark border indicates you're in Edit mode.

② To merge several cells, drag the mouse across the cells to highlight them.

③ Then click the **Merge Cells** button on the Tables and Borders toolbar. The selected cells are combined into one cell.

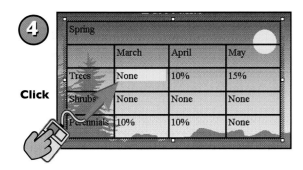

Click

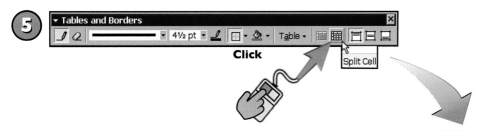

Click

Split Cell

✓ **Displaying the Tables and Borders Toolbar**
If the Tables and Borders toolbar does not appear when you click the table, you can display the toolbar by clicking the **Tables and Borders** button on the Standard toolbar.

✓ **Selecting Cells with the Keyboard**
To select multiple cells with the kybrde the arrow keys to place the flashing cursor in the first cell. Then press **Shift** and the keyboard arrow key that points in the direction you want to highlight.

④ To divide a cell in half, click the cell to make it active.

⑤ Click the **Split Cell** button on the Tables and Borders toolbar. The selected cell is split into two cells.

End Task

Task 8: Formatting Data in a Table

Enhancing the Data in a Table

You can quickly change the appearance of the data in a table by applying text formatting using the **Formatting toolbar**. Additional options are available on the **Drawing** toolbar and the **Tables and Borders** toolbar.

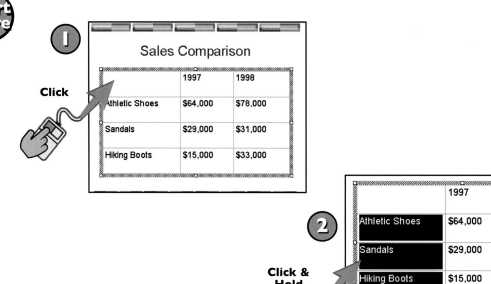

Start Here

Click

Sales Comparison

	1997	1998
Athletic Shoes	$64,000	$78,000
Sandals	$29,000	$31,000
Hiking Boots	$15,000	$33,000

Click & Hold

	1997	1998
Athletic Shoes	$64,000	$78,000
Sandals	$29,000	$31,000
Hiking Boots	$15,000	$33,000

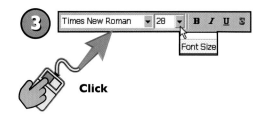

Click

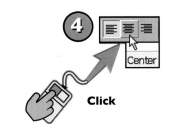

Click

✓ Selecting Data

Double-click to select one item in a cell. Triple-click to select the contents of the entire cell. You can also drag the mouse pointer across data to select part of a cell or across cells to select multiple cells.

1. Click anywhere inside the table to edit the table. The slash mark border indicates you're in Edit mode.

2. Select the data or cells you want to format.

3. To change the font and font size or to apply bold, italic, or underline, click the buttons on the Formatting toolbar.

4. To adjust the horizontal alignment, click the **Align Left**, **Align Center** or **Align Right** buttons on the Formatting toolbar.

Next Step

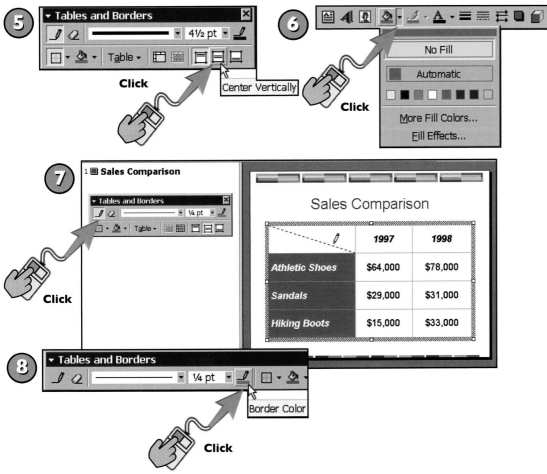

⑤ To adjust the vertical alignment, click the **Align Top**, **Center Vertically**, or **Align Bottom** buttons on the Tables and Borders toolbar.

⑥ To change the font color or cell color, click the **Font Color** or **Fill Color** buttons on the Drawing toolbar.

⑦ Click the **Draw Table** button on the Tables and Borders toolbar to create split cells, to add more rows and columns to a table, or to draw diagonal lines in a cell.

⑧ Click the border line thickness or line color buttons on the Tables and Borders toolbar to further modify the table borders.

End Task

✓ Change Your Mind?
If you decide you don't like the formatting you've applied, you can choose **Edit, Undo.** The Undo command typically retains the last 20 changes you made. Repeat **Undo** until the formatting is restored.

✓ Formatting Borders
See Part 8, Task 9 to learn how to format the borders and gridlines in a table.

Changing Border Line and Background Color in a Table

You can make a table stand out clearly from the rest of the slide by making some simple formatting changes.

Task 9: Applying Border Formatting and Shading to a Table

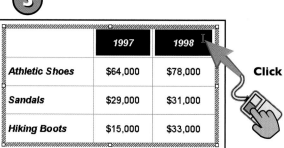

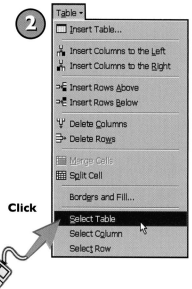

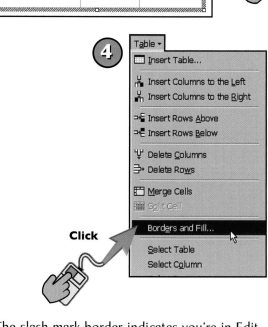

✓ **Buttons on the Tables and Borders Toolbar**
Some of the buttons on the Tables and Borders toolbar can be used to format the table border lines and background color.

1 Click anywhere inside the table to edit the table. The slash mark border indicates you're in Edit mode.

2 To format the entire table, choose **Table**, **Select Table** from the Tables and Borders toolbar.

3 To format only a few cells, hold and drag the mouse pointer across the cells to select them.

4 Choose **Table**, **Borders and Fill** from the Tables and Borders toolbar.

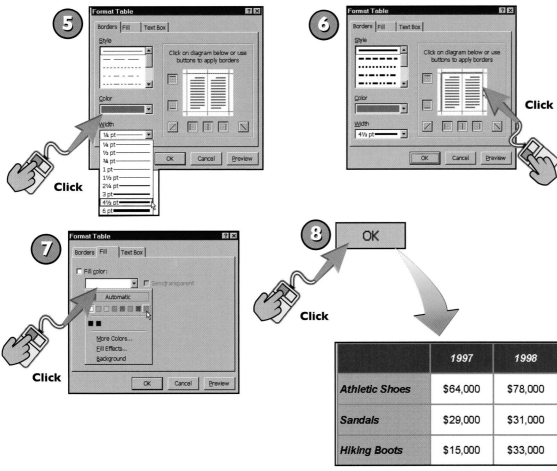

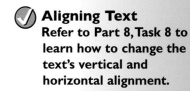

	1997	1998
Athletic Shoes	$64,000	$78,000
Sandals	$29,000	$31,000
Hiking Boots	$15,000	$33,000

5 On the **Borders** tab of the Format Table dialog box, choose the border **Style**, **Color**, and **Width** you want to apply to the selected cells.

6 Click the diagram to indicate the borders that you want to change.

7 To apply a background color to the selected cells, click the **Fill** tab and choose a color from the drop-down list.

8 Click **OK** to apply the changes to the table.

✔️ **Aligning Text**
Refer to Part 8, Task 8 to learn how to change the text's vertical and horizontal alignment.

Sharing Data with Other Microsoft Office Programs

One of the most useful and timesaving features of Office programs is the ease with which you can use the data from one program in another program. You can import a spreadsheet from Excel or a paragraph of text from Word into PowerPoint slides, eliminating the need to retype the data. You can also export a PowerPoint slide so you can use it in another program, such as Word.

This part concentrates on the most common importing and exporting tasks you will need to use. In most cases, you can create a link between the program where the data originated (the source) and the program with which the data is to be shared (the target). The advantage of creating a link is that when the data changes in the source program, it is changed in the target program automatically.

Tasks

Displaying Excel Data in PowerPoint Slides

You can import data from an Excel spreadsheet into PowerPoint. You can link the PowerPoint slide to the original Excel data so the information on the slide automatically updates when you change the data in Excel.

Task 1: Importing Data from an Excel Spreadsheet

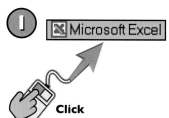
Start Here

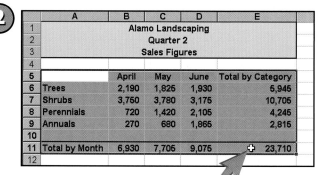

① Microsoft Excel

Click

②

	A	B	C	D	E
1		Alamo Landscaping			
2		Quarter 2			
3		Sales Figures			
4					
5		April	May	June	Total by Category
6	Trees	2,190	1,825	1,930	5,945
7	Shrubs	3,750	3,780	3,175	10,705
8	Perennials	720	1,420	2,105	4,245
9	Annuals	270	680	1,865	2,815
10					
11	Total by Month	6,930	7,705	9,075	23,710
12					

Click & Hold

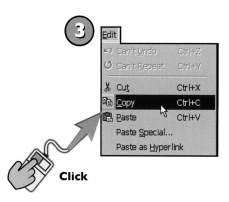

③ Edit

↶ Can't Undo	Ctrl+Z	
↷ Can't Repeat	Ctrl+Y	
✂ Cut	Ctrl+X	
🗐 Copy	Ctrl+C	
🗐 Paste	Ctrl+V	
Paste Special...		
Paste as Hyperlink		

Click

④ Microsoft PowerPoint...

Click

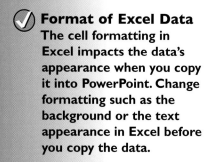

✓ Format of Excel Data
The cell formatting in Excel impacts the data's appearance when you copy it into PowerPoint. Change formatting such as the background or the text appearance in Excel before you copy the data.

① Open or switch to the Excel file that contains the data you want to import.

② Hold and drag the mouse pointer across the cells to select the data you want to copy into PowerPoint.

③ Choose **Edit**, **Copy**.

④ Switch back to PowerPoint and the slide into which you want to import the data.

Next Step

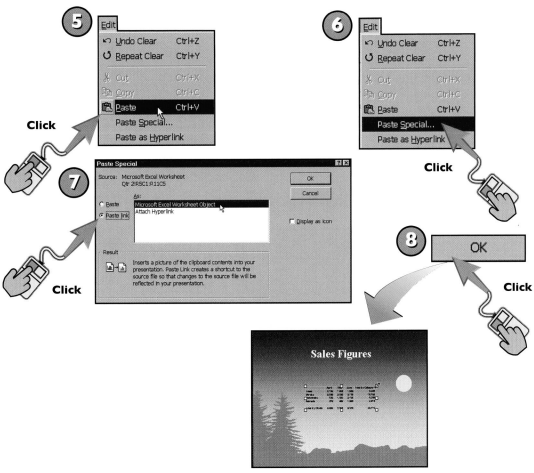

Click

Click

Click

Click

Sales Figures

End
Task

5️⃣ Choose **Edit**, **Paste** to copy the data into the PowerPoint slide. (If you choose this command, skip the rest of the steps in this task.)

6️⃣ Or choose **Edit**, **Paste Special**.

7️⃣ Then click **Paste Link** and then click **Microsoft Excel Worksheet Object** to have the PowerPoint slide automatically update when the Excel data changes.

8️⃣ Click **OK**. The Excel data displays in the PowerPoint slide. Move and resize the object as necessary.

✅ **Paste Versus Paste Special**
If you choose **Paste** instead of **Paste Special** (or **Paste Link**), the data in the PowerPoint slide does not change when you update the data in Excel.

✅ **Move and Resize the Imported Object**
Refer to Part 5, Tasks 2 and 3 for steps to move and resize the data imported from Excel.

✅ **Importing Data into a Chart**
See Part 6, Task 5 for steps on importing Excel data into a PowerPoint graphic chart.

Task 2: Importing an Outline from Word

Start Here

Converting a Word File into a PowerPoint Presentation

Before you can create a PowerPoint presentation from a Word outline, you must format the outline in a way PowerPoint can understand. Use the built-in Heading styles in Word to organize the text. Heading 1 text becomes slide titles, Heading 2 text becomes first level bullets, Heading 3 text becomes second level bullets, and so forth. If you simply want to copy data from Word into PowerPoint, use the **Edit, Copy** and **Edit, Paste** commands.

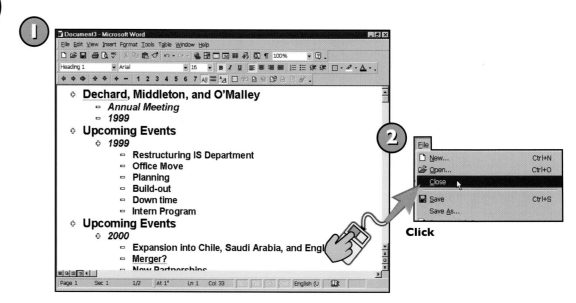

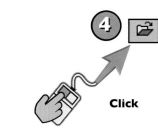
Click

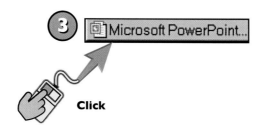
Click

Click

1. Create the Word outline by using the Outline view in Word or by applying Heading styles to each level in the outline.

2. Choose **File**, **Close**. The Word file must be closed before you can import it into PowerPoint.

3. Open or switch to PowerPoint.

4. In PowerPoint, click the **Open** button on the Standard toolbar.

Next Step

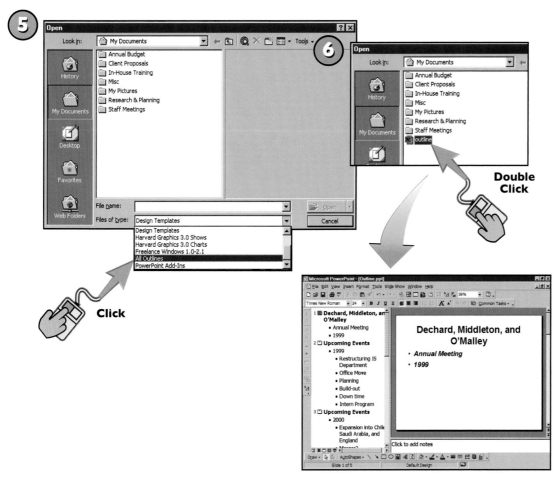

In the Open dialog box, choose **All Outlines** from the **Files of type** drop-down list.

Locate and double-click the Word file. A new PowerPoint presentation is created from the text in the Word file.

Locating the Word Document
If the Word file is not in the My Documents folder, use the **Look in** drop-down box to locate the file.

Task 3: Importing a Table from Word

Bringing a Word Table into PowerPoint

Copying a table from Word and pasting it into a PowerPoint slide is accomplished with just a few mouse clicks!

Start Here

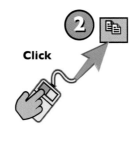

1

Alamo Landscaping – News & Notes

Discounts: Our busy season is approaching and we will be offering our customers discounts on certain items. During the months of April, May, and June we will be advertising these discounts in the local paper. Make sure you know which items are discounted and which ones are not. Reminders will be posted at the beginning of each month. Discounts are never offered on Japanese Maples or Dogwoods.

You will notice that Annuals will not be discounted during this period. They will be discounted during the July-September period.

	April	May	June
Trees	10%	15%	25%
Shrubs	None	None	10%
Perennials	10%	None	10%

Employee Benefits: We are pleased to announce that full-time employees are eligible for dental care coverage, as part of our new health care pa...

Click & Drag

2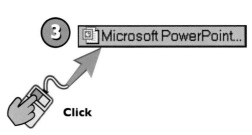

Click

3 🗐 Microsoft PowerPoint...

Click

4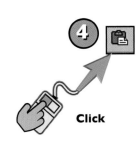

Click

✔ Creating Tables in PowerPoint

Instead of creating a table in Word and copying it into PowerPoint, you can create a table directly in PowerPoint. Refer to Part 8 for steps on creating and formatting tables.

1 In Word, select the table you want to import into PowerPoint.

2 Click the **Copy** button.

3 Switch back to PowerPoint and display the slide in which you want the Word table displayed.

4 Click the **Paste** button. The Word table appears in the PowerPoint slide.

Next Step

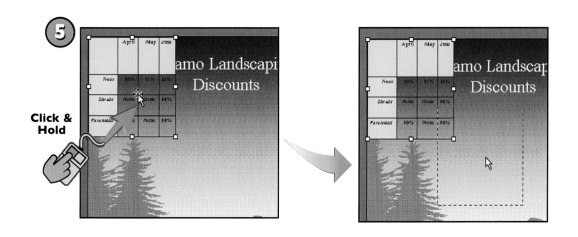

Click & Hold

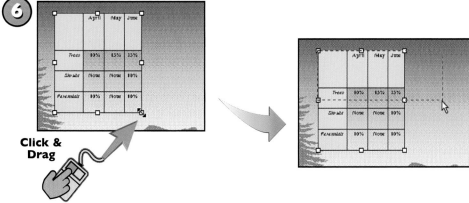

Click & Drag

(5) Click and hold the mouse pointer in the middle of the table to move it.

(6) Drag a corner selection handle to resize the Word table.

✓ **Formatting the Text**
Refer to Part 5, Task 8 for steps to format the object text.

✓ **Linking the Table to PowerPoint**
Alternatively, you can use the **Edit, Paste Special, Paste Link** command to link the Word table to PowerPoint. When the data in the Word table changes, the copy of the table in PowerPoint will immediately reflect those changes.

End Task

Copying a PowerPoint Slide to a Word Document

You can incorporate a PowerPoint slide into a Word document by using the **Copy** and **Paste** commands.

Copying PowerPoint Slides

These same steps can be used to copy a PowerPoint slide into programs other than Word.

Task 4: Exporting a PowerPoint Slide to a Word Document

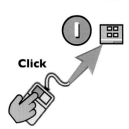

Click

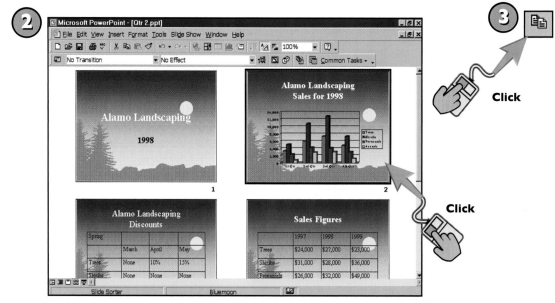

Click

Click

 Click the **Slide Sorter View** button in the lower-left corner of the PowerPoint screen.

 Click the slide you want to copy. A heavy, dark border appears around the selected slide.

 Click the **Copy** button.

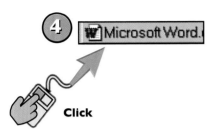

Click

Click

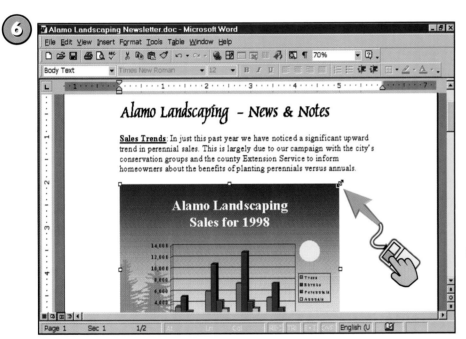

Click & Drag

④ Open or switch to Word.

⑤ Click the **Paste** button.

⑥ Click the slide object. Use corner selection handles to resize it as necessary.

Linking the PowerPoint Slide If you want to link the PowerPoint slide to Word, use **Edit, Paste Special, Paste Link** to create the link. When the slide is changed in PowerPoint, it will be updated in the Word document automatically.

End Task

Printing Your Presentation

PowerPoint enables you to print your presentation slides exactly as they appear in the Slide Show. You can also print the text displayed in the Outline pane, notes created in the Notes pane, or audience handouts showing miniatures of your slides.

To save time, you can choose to print multiple copies of your slides, handouts, outline text, or notes pages. You can print draft copies in black-and-white so you can save color for your final printouts.

The Print dialog box is where you select what you want to print. This dialog box can only be accessed through the File menu; it does not display when you select the Print button on the Standard toolbar.

Tasks

Task 1: Printing Slides

Setting Options to Print a Copy of Your Slides

Using the Print dialog box, you can print all or only a few of the presentation slides, choose the number of copies to print, and print draft copies in black-and-white.

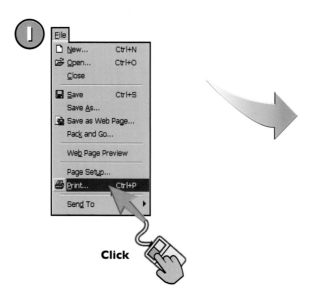

Click

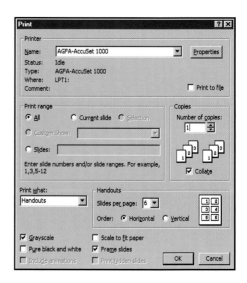

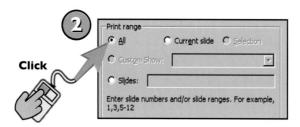

Click

1 To print the active presentation, choose **File**, **Print**. The Print dialog box opens. Use it to choose what you want to print. The default options are shown.

2 Choose an option in the **Print Range** area—print all slides, print only the current slide, print specific slides selected in the Slide Sorter view, or print individual slide numbers you specify.

Next Step

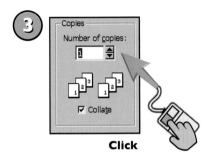

Click

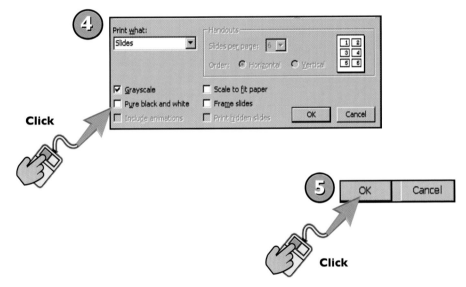

Click

Click

WARNING
If you click the **Print** button on the Standard toolbar, your slides are printed immediately, using the default settings. The Print dialog box does not appear.

Printing Black-and-White Slides
The **Grayscale** setting prints in shades of gray. **Pure black and white** prints in only black-and-white, with no gray shading.

Getting Help
Click the **Help** button (the question mark button in the upper-right corner of the dialog box), and then click on any option in the dialog box to learn more about it.

3 Select the **Number of copies**. Choose whether to have the copies **Collated**.

4 The default **Print what** option is already set to print **Slides**. If you are printing draft copies, choose either **Grayscale** or **Pure black and white**.

5 Click **OK** to print the slides.

Choosing Options for Printing Handout Pages

You can print handouts that display two, three, four, six, or nine slides on each printed page. When you print three slides per page, PowerPoint also prints lines next to the slides for the audience to take notes.

Task 2: Printing Handouts for Your Audience

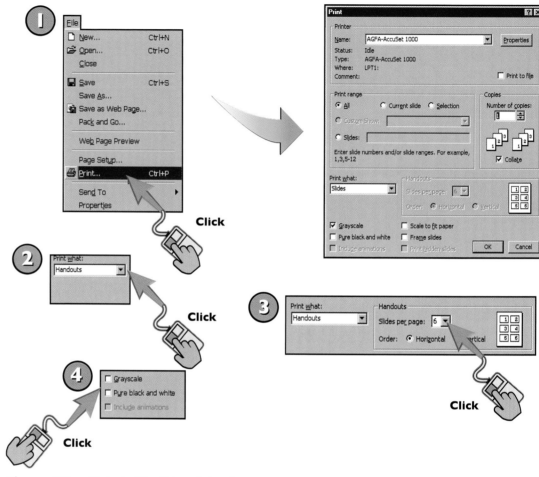

✓ **You Must Use the Dialog Box to Print Handouts**

You cannot print handouts by using the **Print** button or the **Ctrl+P** keyboard shortcut. You must use the Print dialog box.

① Choose **File**, **Print**. The Print dialog box appears.

② From the **Print what** drop-down list, choose the **Handouts** option.

③ In the **Slides per page** drop-down list, choose the number of slides to print per page. Also, click the Horizontal or Vertical radio button to choose the order in which to print the slides.

④ To print draft handouts, select **Grayscale** or **Pure black and white**. If you have a black-and-white printer, selecting Grayscale prints clearer handouts.

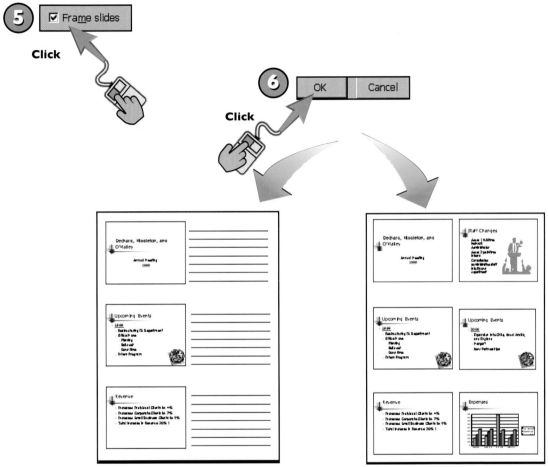

5 Click

6 Click

| OK | Cancel |

Adding Headers and Footers to Handouts Choose **View, Master, Handout Master** to add headers and footers, such as the date the handout was printed, the name and phone number of the presenter, or to set the page number to include the total page count (for example, Page 1 of 5).

Choosing a Handout Option The Handout option with three slides per page is a favorite among audiences. These handouts print three slide miniatures along the left side of each page and lines for taking notes along the right side.

5 By default, the **Frame slides** option prints handouts with a thin border around each slide. Uncheck this option if you do not want the border.

6 Choose **OK** to print the handouts. Handouts with three slides per page include space for notes. Handouts with six slides per page are great for long presentations—it saves paper.

Task 3: Printing the Presentation Outline

Printing the Outline Pane

The text displayed in the Outline pane is the bulk of most presentations. Having a printout of this text provides an easy way to review the presentation's flow and tone. You can print the full outline or collapse the outline to only the slide titles.

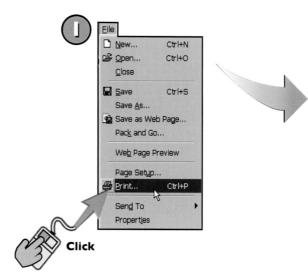

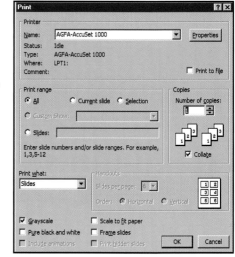

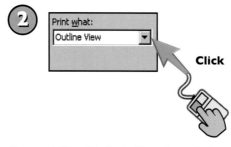

✓ **Outline Pane Text**
The only text you see in the Outline pane is text that is part of a "click" placeholder. Independent text, graphic charts, tables, and picture clips do not appear in the Outline pane.

① Choose **File**, **Print**. The Print dialog box appears.

② From the **Print what** drop-down list, choose **Outline View**.

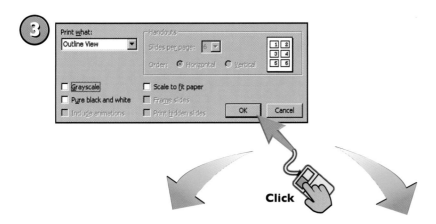

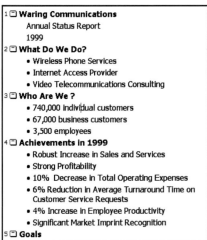

Click

End
Task

③ Choose **OK** to print the outline. If the outline is collapsed when you print it, the printed outline will be collapsed. Otherwise the full outline is printed.

 WARNING
You must use the **Print** dialog box to print the outline. You cannot print the outline by using the **Print** button or the **Ctrl+P** keyboard shortcut.

 Collapsing the Outline
To print only the slide titles, you need to collapse the outline. Choose **View, Toolbars, Outlining.** The Outline toolbar appears next to the Outline pane. Click anywhere in the Outline pane. Then click the **Collapse All** button.

Task 4: Printing Speaker's Notes

Printing the Notes Pages

It is useful to have a set of notes you can refer to when giving a presentation. Notes pages show a miniature of the slide along with the notes for that slide. The Notes Page view provides a preview of the printed speaker's notes.

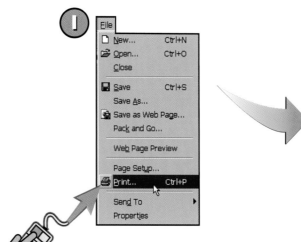

Click

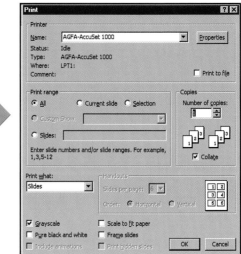

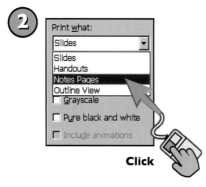

Click

✓ **Creating Speaker's Notes**
Refer to Part 2, Task 3 for the steps to create a set of speaker's notes.

1. Choose **File**, **Print**. The Print dialog box appears.

2. From the **Print what** drop-down list, choose **Notes Pages**.

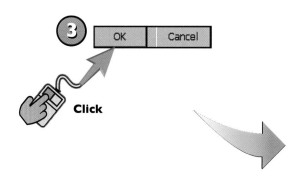

Click

3 Click **OK**. The speaker's notes are printed.

WARNING
You cannot print the notes pages by using the **Print** button or the **Ctrl+P** keyboard shortcut. You must use the Print dialog box.

Displaying the Notes Pages View
Choose **View, Notes Pages** to preview how each printed notes page will appear.

Using the Notes Master
You can add headers and footers to the speaker's notes using the Notes Master. Choose **View, Master, Notes Master** to display the Notes Master.

Selecting Presentation, Animation, and Sound Settings

If you'll be giving presentations using an overhead projection system or running them online, you can improve the delivery of your presentations greatly by adding a few simple enhancements. Choose the way your slides transition from one to another and how long each slide displays. Have a sound (such as applause or screeching tires) play when a specific slide appears. You can also select the order and way in which slide objects appear; for example, each bullet in a list can be displayed separately. Picture clips, WordArt, and drawn objects can be animated to spiral or swivel when they appear onscreen. Even graphic charts can be displayed one series or one category at a time.

You can insert and use the video and sound clips that are available on the Microsoft Office 2000 CD as part of your presentation.

Tasks

Task 1: Previewing Your Presentation

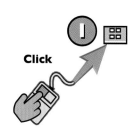

Running the Slide Show

When you add animation and sound to your slides, be sure to preview your presentation to see how the settings look and sound. Previewing a presentation is also known as running the slide show.

Click

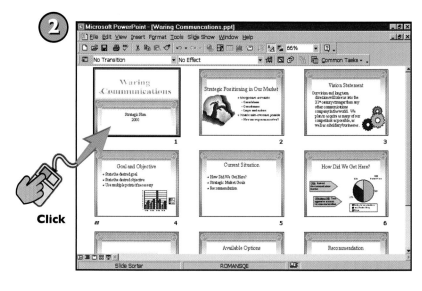

Click

Click

✓ **Displaying Slide Show Settings**

You can run the slide show from any view in PowerPoint. The Slide Sorter view, however, is the only view in which you can display slide show settings (which are discussed later in this part).

1. One way to preview a presentation is to look at the slides in the Slide Sorter view. Click the **Slide Sorter View** button in the lower-left corner of the PowerPoint screen.

2. Another way to preview a presentation is to use the slide show feature. The slide show begins on the active slide, so click the first slide in the presentation.

3. Then click the **Slide Show** button in the lower-left corner of the PowerPoint screen to preview the presentation.

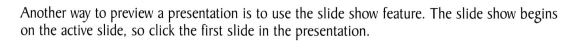

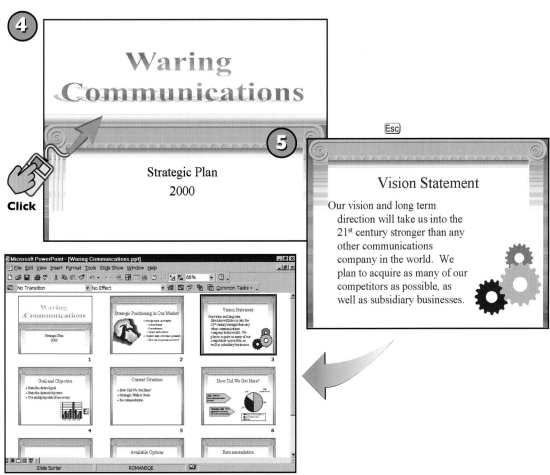

④ Click to display the next slide in the presentation. When you reach the end, you return to the Slide Sorter view.

⑤ To stop the slide show before you reach the end, press **Esc**. You return to the view from which you started the preview, and the last slide you looked at becomes the active slide.

✓ **Why Use the Slide Show?**
Use the slide show feature to preview your presentation before printing, to preview animation settings, and to rehearse your presentation.

Selecting the Way Slides Appear When You Run a Slide Show

One way to make your presentation more interesting is to add slide transition effects. Slide transitions are the way each slide appears as you advance through a presentation.

✓ **Using Transitions Effectively**

When faced with a lengthy presentation, try applying a different transition to each major topic in your presentation. This provides a subtle way of letting the audience know you are discussing a new topic.

Task 2: Adding Transitions Between Slides

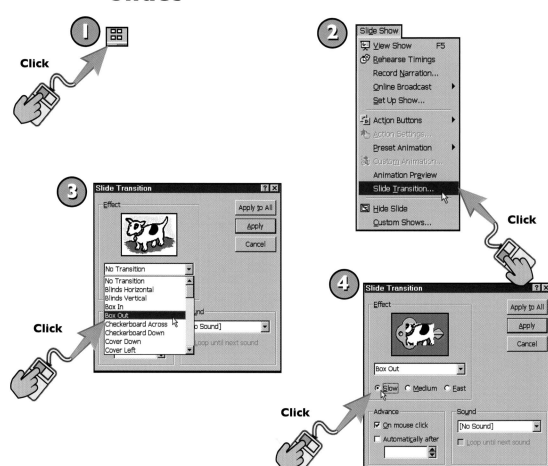

Switch to the Slide Sorter view.

To apply a slide transition, choose **Slide Show**, **Slide Transition**. The Slide Transition dialog box appears.

From the **Effect** drop-down list, choose a transition. The transition is displayed in the preview sample.

Click **Slow**, **Medium**, or **Fast** to set the speed of the transition. The sample changes to illustrate the speed.

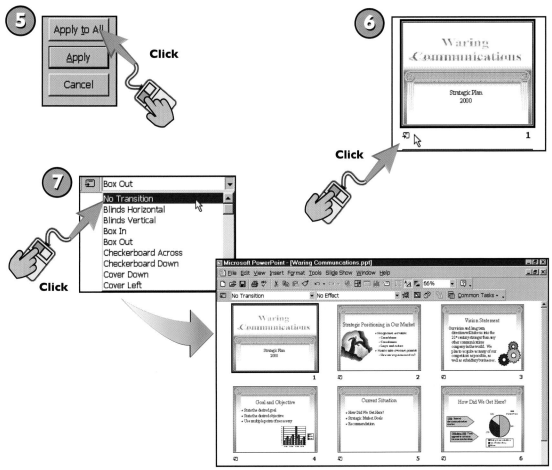

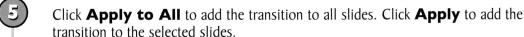

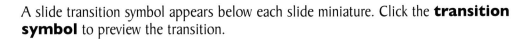

Click

Click

Click

Click

⑤ Click **Apply to All** to add the transition to all slides. Click **Apply** to add the transition to the selected slides.

⑥ A slide transition symbol appears below each slide miniature. Click the **transition symbol** to preview the transition.

⑦ To remove the transition from a slide, select the slide. Then click the transition drop-down list on the Slide Sorter toolbar and choose **No Transition**.

✓ Selecting Multiple Slides
You can select several slides in the Slide Sorter view by clicking the first slide and then holding the **Ctrl** key and clicking each additional slide.

✓ No Transition on the First Slide
Your first slide does not need a transition. It should already be displayed as the audience comes into the room before you begin the presentation.

End Task

Using Transition Sounds

In addition to applying a slide transition effect, you can attach a sound to a slide. As the slide transitions onto the screen, the sound plays. So your audience can hear the transition sounds, make sure the machine you are using to give your presentation is capable of playing sound and has a set of speakers.

Task 3: Adding Sound to the Slide Transitions

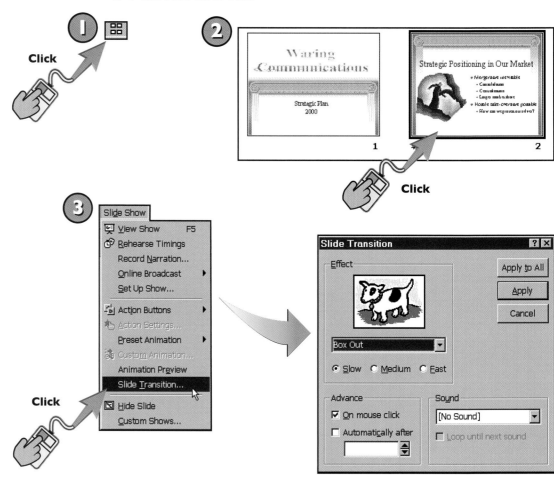

Click

Click

Click

✔ **Repeating Sound Clips**
The Slide Transition dialog box includes an option for the sound to repeat (loop) until the next sound is played.

1 Switch to the Slide Sorter view.

2 Select the slide to which you want to add the sound. A thick border appears around the slide.

3 Choose **Slide Show**, **Slide Transition**. The Slide Transition dialog box appears.

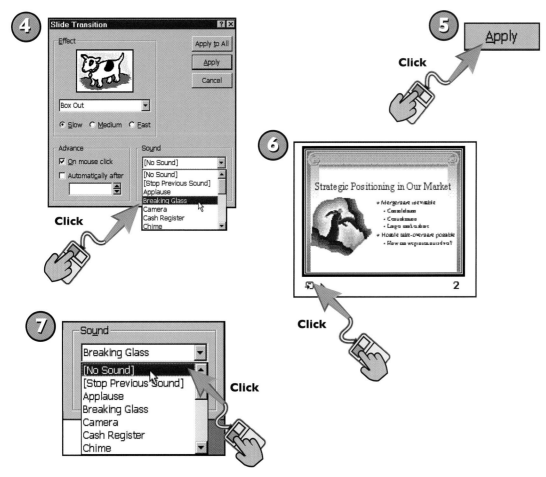

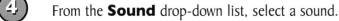

4 From the **Sound** drop-down list, select a sound.

5 Click **Apply**; the sound is attached to the selected slides.

6 Click the transition symbol to see the transition and hear the sound. To add a sound to a slide without a transition, you have to run the slide show to hear the sound.

7 To remove a transition sound, follow Steps 1 to 3. Then from the **Sound** drop-down list, select **No Sound** and click **Apply**.

⚠ WARNING
It is easy to get carried away attaching sounds to slide transitions. **Be sure you have a good reason for adding sound. Audiences might become distracted when too many sounds are used in a presentation—less is better!**

End Task

Task 4: Setting a Display Time on Slides

Using Slide Timings

You can set up your presentation to advance through the slides automatically by adding a display time to each slide. This is particularly useful for standalone presentations at conventions, conferences, and kiosks.

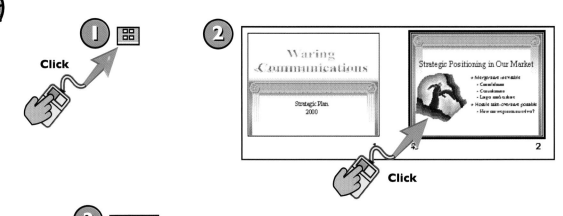

Start Here

Click

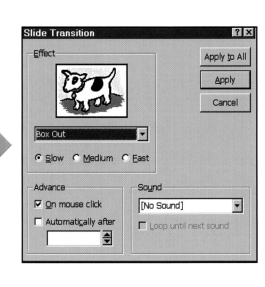

Click

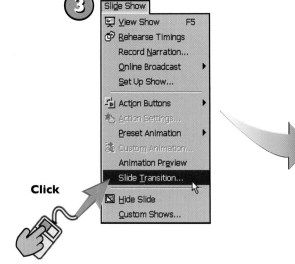

Click

✓ **Pausing a Slide Show**
You can pause (and resume) a timed presentation by pressing the letter **S** on the keyboard. See Part 12, Task 2 (step 6) for a complete list of keyboard shortcuts.

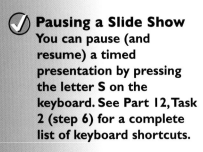

1 Switch to the Slide Sorter view.

2 Select the slide to which you want to apply a display time. A thick border appears around the slide.

3 Choose **Slide Show**, **Slide Transition**. The Slide Transition dialog box appears.

Next Step

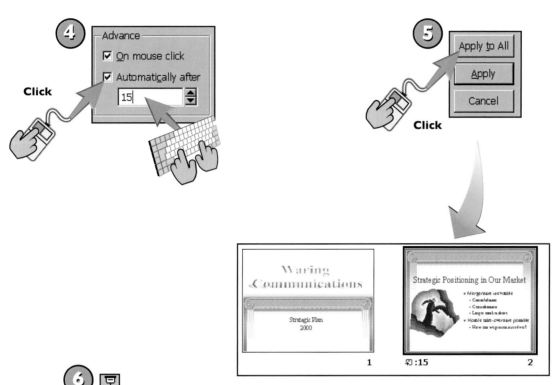

Click

Click

✓ **Running the Presentation in a Continuous Loop**
See Part 12, Task 4 to learn how to set up the presentation to run continuously.

④ Click to check the **Automatically after** option and type the number of seconds you want the slide to be displayed on the screen.

⑤ Click **Apply to All** to add the same time to all slides, or click **Apply** to add the time only to the selected slides. The time appears next to the slide transition symbol.

⑥ Run the slide show to confirm the slide timings.

✓ **Rehearsing a Presentation**
You can practice a presentation to determine how long it will take you. Choose **Slide Show, Rehearse Timings.**

End Task

Task 5: Animating Text

Building the Slide Text

When you run a slide show, you have the option of displaying a bulleted (or numbered) list one bullet (or number) at a time—in effect "building" the slide text. This technique is used to keep your audience focused as you display and discuss each point (or to prevent them from reading ahead). Building slide objects is called *animation*.

Click

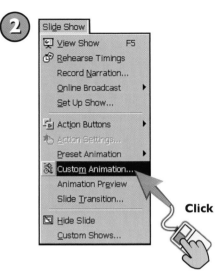

Click

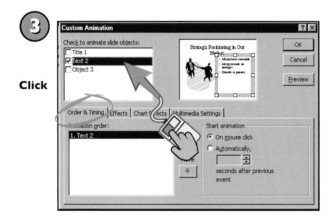

Click

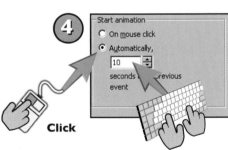

Click

✓ **Custom Animation**
The Custom Animation feature is available only in the Normal and Slide views.

1 Switch to the **Slide** pane in the Normal view or to the Slide view; then display the slide you want to animate.

2 Choose **Slide Show**, **Custom Animation**.

3 From the **Order & Timing** tab, check the object you want to animate. The miniature shows the selected object, and the object appears in the **Animation order** list.

4 To have the text appear at certain timed intervals, click **Automatically** and type the time. Otherwise, click **On mouse click**.

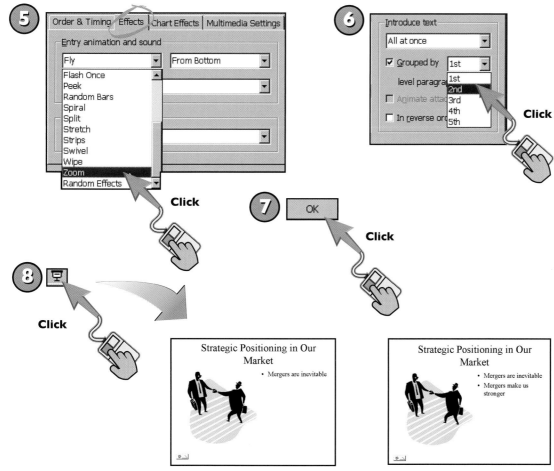

On the **Effects** tab, select an effect from the **Entry animation and sound** drop-down list.

To display each bullet or number separately, choose a level from the **Grouped by** drop-down list.

Click **OK** to apply the animation.

Then click the **Slide Show** button to run the slide show and see the animation.

✓ **Animating Other Objects**
You can animate any slide object—not only the text. See Part 11, Tasks 6 and 7 for steps to animate picture clips, WordArt, drawn objects, and graphic charts.

✓ **Previewing Animation Settings**
In the Custom Animation dialog box, click the **Preview** button to see the animation effects in the slide miniature.

Applying Animation Effects to Slide Objects

In addition to text, other objects can be animated when you run a slide show. A WordArt or picture clip object can spin or spiral in, or a sound can play, as it appears onscreen.

Task 6: Animating Picture Clips, WordArt, and Drawings

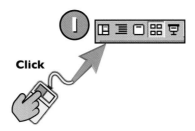

Click

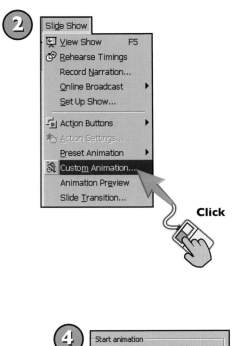

Click

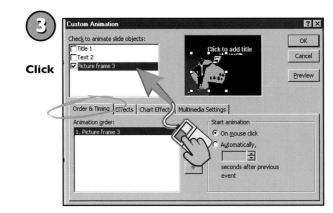

Click

Click

⚠️ **WARNING**

Although animation can liven up any presentation, if you animate every object on a slide, the audience might find it distracting.

 Switch to the **Slide** pane in the Normal view or to the Slide view, and then display the slide you want to animate.

 Choose **Slide Show**, **Custom Animation**.

 From the **Order & Timing** tab, check the object you want to animate. The miniature shows the selected object and the object appears in the **Animation order** list.

 To have the object appear at a timed interval, click **Automatically** and type the time. Otherwise click **On mouse click**.

Next Step

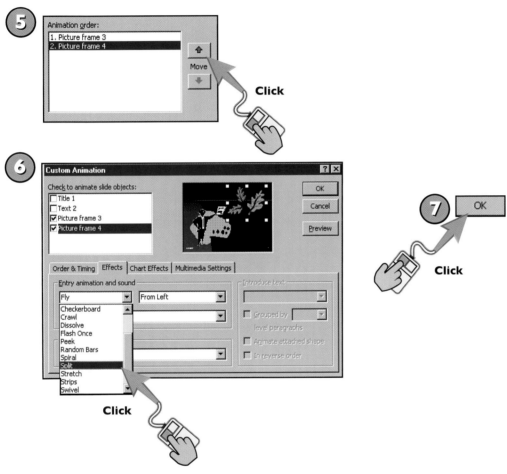

5 If you animate more than one object, you can change the order in which objects animate by selecting an object in the **Animation order** list and using the **Move** arrows.

6 On the **Effects** tab, choose animation and sound effects from the **Entry animation and sound** drop-down lists.

7 Click **OK** to apply the animation settings to the objects.

✅ **Preview Animation Settings**
Click the **Preview** button in the **Custom Animation** dialog box to see the animation effects in the slide miniature.

✅ **Hiding Objects After They Animate**
On the **Effects** tab of the **Custom Animation** dialog box is an option to hide the object after it has animated. Click the **After Animation** drop-down list and choose **Hide After Animation**.

Task 7: Animating Charts

Building Graphic Charts

Animating charts is especially useful when you want to discuss the chart in detail. By displaying the data sequentially, you can be certain of the audience's attention.

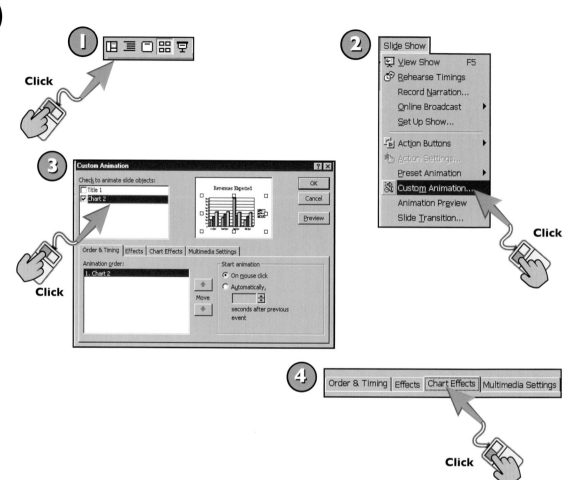

Start Here

Click

Click

Click

Click

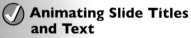 **Animating Slide Titles and Text**

In addition to animating the chart, you can animate the slide title and any other objects in the **Check to animate slide objects** list.

1. Switch to the **Slide** pane in the Normal view or to the Slide view. Then display the slide you want to animate.

2. Choose **Slide Show**, **Custom Animation**.

3. From the **Order & Timing** tab, check the chart you want to animate. The miniature shows the chart as selected and the chart appears in the **Animation order** list.

4. Click the **Chart Effects** tab.

Next Step

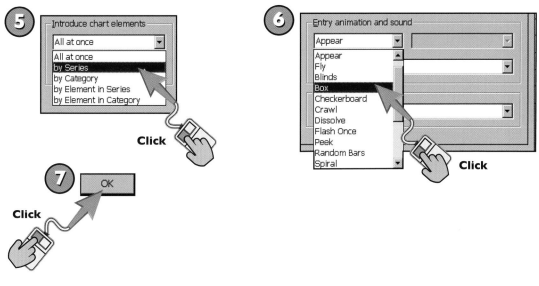

Click

Click

(7) OK

Click

Click **(8)** 🖵

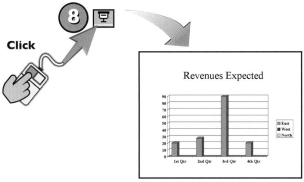

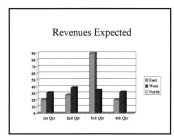

Revenues Expected

Revenues Expected

(5) From the **Introduce chart elements** drop-down list, choose how the chart will be animated—by series, by category, or by data point.

(6) From the **Entry animation and sound** drop-down lists, select the animation and sound effects.

(7) Click **OK** to apply the animation.

(8) Click on the **Slide Show** button in the lower-left corner of the screen to see the animation.

✅ **Chart Animation Choices**
With graphic charts, you can animate by series, by category, or by each data point. In this example the chart is being animated by data series. Expenses and Revenue are the series; the four quarters are the categories.

✅ **Avoid Sound Effects with Chart Animation**
Reserve sound effects for text, picture clips, WordArt, or drawn objects.

End Task

Running Your Presentation

After you develop a presentation, you can print it or run it as a slide show. A **slide show** is simply a presentation you can run on a monitor or overhead projection system for an audience to view. You can set options for your presentation so you can loop the presentation continuously or run it with set display times for each slide.

While you run the slide show, you can easily skip slides or go back to an earlier slide. Additionally, you can take minutes (or notes) and assign action items as the presentation progresses. These minutes and assignments can be exported into Microsoft Word or Outlook.

The presentation can be saved as an HTML (Hypertext Markup Language) file so it can be viewed in a Web browser on the Internet or on your company's intranet.

Tasks

Selecting Slide Show Settings and Running the Slide Show

Before running the slide show, you might want to confirm or change the slide show settings.

Task 1: Running a Slide Show

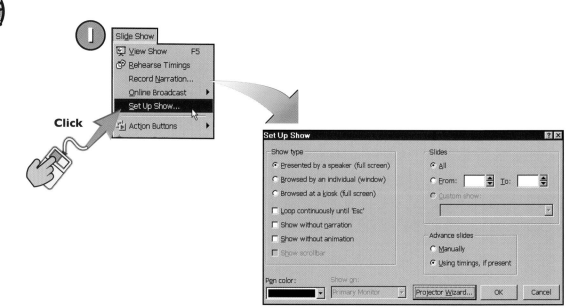

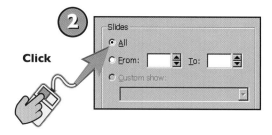

Click

Running the Slide Show

If you run the slide show without first validating the settings, the default settings are used.

① Choose **Slide Show**, **Set Up Show**. The Set Up Show dialog box appears. This dialog box contains several options you can set before running the slide show.

② By default, all slides in the presentation are displayed when you run the slide show. You have the option of designating a range of slides to be displayed.

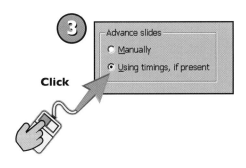

Click

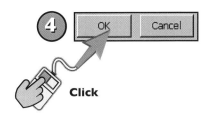

Click

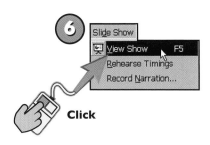

Click

✔ **Rehearsing the Slide Show**
If you have a limited amount of time to give your presentation, consider rehearsing it. Time yourself or add a display time to each slide; the slide show runs using the timings, automatically changing to the next slide. To rehearse your presentation, choose **Slide Show, Rehearse Timings. Refer to Part 11, Task 4** to set a display time on each slide.

(3) Make sure the **Using timings, if present** option is selected if you have set a display time on the presentation slides.

(4) Click **OK** to accept the slide show settings.

(5) To run the slide show from the active slide, click the **Slide Show** button in the lower-left corner of the screen.

(6) To run the slide show from the first slide in the presentation, choose **Slide Show, View Show**.

Moving Around in the Presentation While Running the Slide Show

While running a slide show, it is sometimes necessary to skip forward or jump back to a particular slide. If the slides have predefined timings, you might want to pause the show as you (or the audience) discuss a slide topic in more depth. You can use the **Slide Navigator** or keyboard shortcuts to move around during a slide show.

Task 2: Navigating Through a Presentation

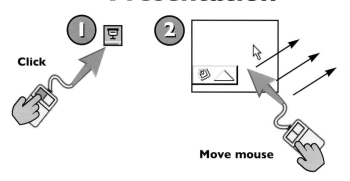

Click

Move mouse

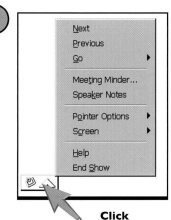

Click

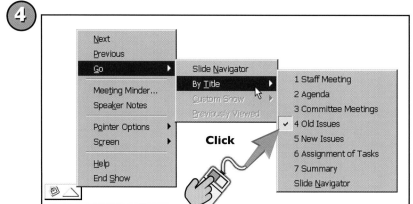

Click

① After you establish the slide show settings (described in Part 12, Task 1), start the **Slide Show**.

② When you move the mouse during the Slide Show, the Slide Show control appears in the lower-left corner of the screen.

③ Click the **Slide Show control** to display a list of commands available while the show is running.

④ Display a specific slide by choosing **Go**, **By Title** from the **Slide Show control** menu. Then select the slide you want to display.

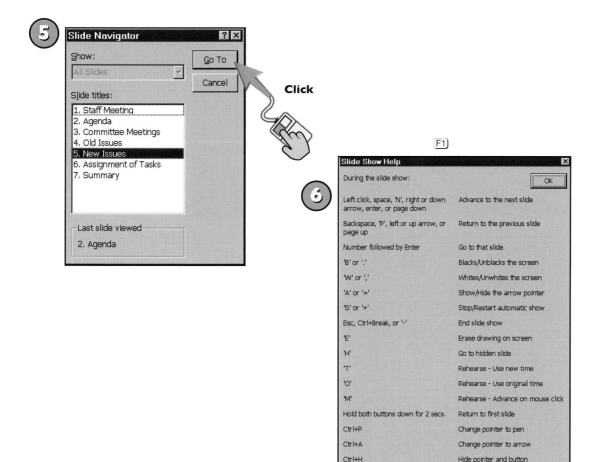

Slide Navigator

Show:
All Slides

Go To
Cancel

Click

Slide titles:

1. Staff Meeting
2. Agenda
3. Committee Meetings
4. Old Issues
5. New Issues
6. Assignment of Tasks
7. Summary

Last slide viewed
2. Agenda

F1

Slide Show Help

During the slide show:

OK

Left click, space, 'N', right or down arrow, enter, or page down	Advance to the next slide
Backspace, 'P', left or up arrow, or page up	Return to the previous slide
Number followed by Enter	Go to that slide
'B' or '.'	Blacks/Unblacks the screen
'W' or ','	Whites/Unwhites the screen
'A' or '='	Show/Hide the arrow pointer
'S' or '+'	Stop/Restart automatic show
Esc, Ctrl+Break, or '-'	End slide show
'E'	Erase drawing on screen
'H'	Go to hidden slide
'T'	Rehearse - Use new time
'O'	Rehearse - Use original time
'M'	Rehearse - Advance on mouse click
Hold both buttons down for 2 secs.	Return to first slide
Ctrl+P	Change pointer to pen
Ctrl+A	Change pointer to arrow
Ctrl+H	Hide pointer and button
Ctrl+U	Automatically show/hide pointer and

⑤ Or from the **Slide Show control** menu, choose **Go**, **Slide Navigator**. Then select the slide title and choose **Go To**.

⑥ You can also use keyboard shortcuts to navigate through a slide show. While running the slide show, press **F1** to see a list of keyboard shortcuts.

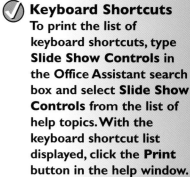

✓ Keyboard Shortcuts
To print the list of keyboard shortcuts, type **Slide Show Controls** in the **Office Assistant** search box and select **Slide Show Controls** from the list of help topics. With the keyboard shortcut list displayed, click the **Print** button in the help window.

✓ Shortcut to Display the Slide Show Control Menu
The **Slide Show control** menu also appears if you right-click any part of the slide while running the show.

End Task

Task 3: Using the Meeting Minder

Taking Notes and Assigning Tasks During a Slide Show

While running the Slide Show, you can use the Meeting Minder to document meeting minutes and action items and to export the minutes and action items to Word or Outlook.

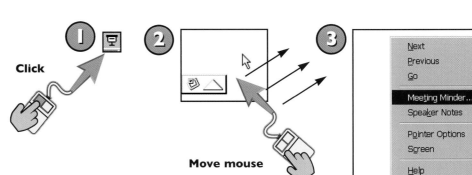

✓ **Scheduling an Outlook Appointment**
The **Schedule** button in the Meeting Minder starts Outlook and displays an appointment window.

1 After establishing the slide show settings (described in Part 12, Task 1), start the **Slide Show**.

2 When you move the mouse during the Slide Show, the **Slide Show control** appears in the lower-left corner of the screen.

3 Choose **Meeting Minder** from the **Slide Show control** menu.

4 To create minutes or notes during slide show discussions, type the minutes in the Meeting Minutes text box.

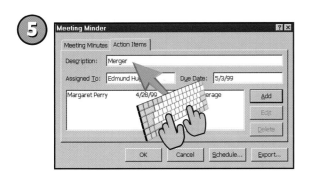

Click

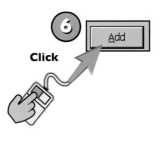

Click

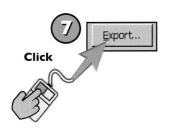

Click

Click

Assigned To Text Limitation
The maximum number of characters allowed in the Assigned To box is 15.

Export to Outlook or Word
The **Export** button lets you export the action items to **Outlook**, export the minutes and action items to **Word**, or export to both programs.

5 To create action items, type the action description, assignment, and date due on the **Action Items** tab of the Meeting Minder dialog box.

6 Click **Add**. PowerPoint adds a slide listing the action items to the end of the presentation.

7 Click the **Export** button.

8 After selecting one or both of the **Export options**, click **Export Now**.

Running the Slide Show in an Automatic Loop

In some situations, it is useful to have a slide show run automatically, without the need to restart the show each time. This is especially useful at conferences, trade shows, and kiosks.

Task 4: Setting the Presentation to Run Continuously

Click

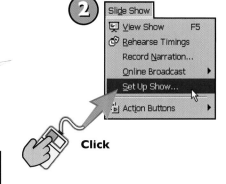

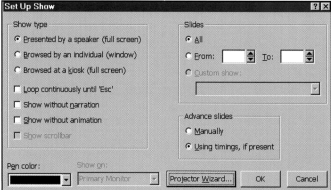

Click

 **WARNING**

When you're running a presentation in a continuous loop, you must have display times assigned to each slide. Refer to Part 11, Task 4 for steps on adding automatic display times to slides.

 Open or switch to the presentation you want to run continuously.

 Choose **Slide Show**, **Set Up Show**. The Set Up Show dialog box appears.

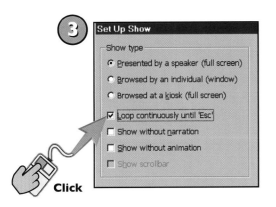

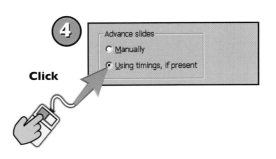

Click

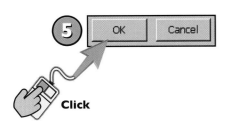

Click

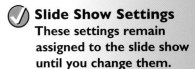

Click

3) Choose **Loop continuously until 'Esc'**.

4) Make sure the **Using timings, if present** option is selected.

5) Click **OK**.

6) When you are ready to run the show continuously, click the **Slide Show** button. Press **Esc** to stop the show.

✓ **Slide Show Settings**
These settings remain assigned to the slide show until you change them.

✓ **Advancing the Slide Show**
You must set the slides to advance by using the slide timings; otherwise, the person viewing the show has to press **Enter** or click the mouse to advance the show.

Saving a Presentation as an HTML File

If you want the presentation to be shown on your company's intranet or on the Internet, it needs to be in a special file format called **HTML**—Hypertext Markup Language. Once saved in this format, the presentation can be viewed using a browser, such as Internet Explorer or Netscape Navigator.

Task 5: Setting the Presentation to Run on a Network

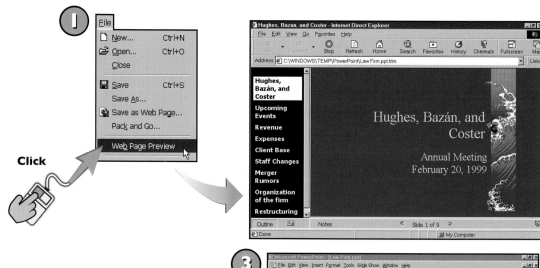

Click

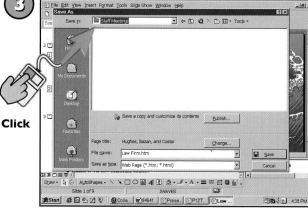

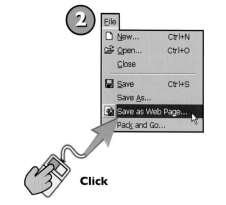

Click

Click

1 Open or switch to the presentation you want to run on a network. Then choose **File**, **Web Page Preview** to see how the presentation will appear in a browser.

2 Close the browser window. Then choose **File**, **Save as Web Page**.

3 In the Save As dialog box, use the **Save in** drop-down list or **Places Bar** to locate the folder you want to save the presentation in; you can store it in the default folder.

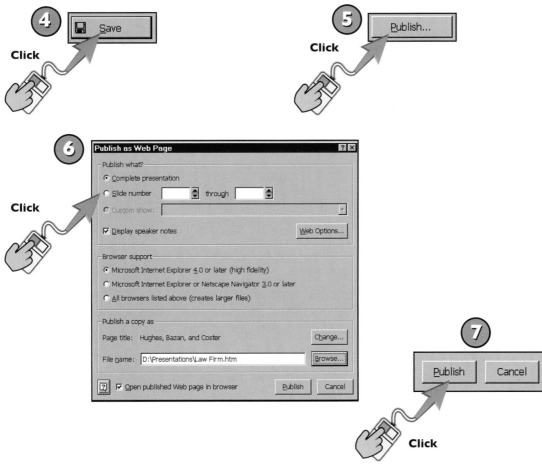

4 Click **Save**.

5 If you want to store the presentation as a Web Page on a Web server, click the **Publish** button in the Save As dialog box.

6 In the Publish as Web Page dialog box, choose the settings for what you want to publish, the browser option to use, and the location of the server where you want the files stored.

7 Click **Publish**.

 Saving Versus Publishing
When you save a presentation as a Web page, PowerPoint converts it to an HTML file format. When you publish a presentation, you not only save it in the HTML format, but also establish the browser and other file settings and store the file on a Web server, where it can be viewed as a Web site.

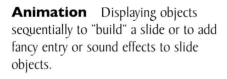

Animation   Displaying objects sequentially to "build" a slide or to add fancy entry or sound effects to slide objects.

Branch (Organization chart) A manager box and all the subordinate boxes.

Browser   Software you use to view Web sites. Microsoft Internet Explorer and Netscape Navigator are the most common browsers.

Bullets   A list of individual text topics or points.

Cell   The intersection of a row and column in a chart's Datasheet or in a table.

"Click" placeholder   A predefined object in a PowerPoint slide, such as a title, a list of bullets, or a graphic chart.

Current cell   The active cell in a chart's Datasheet or in a table. Typically, a flashing cursor appears in the current cell.

Data category   A group of data points, one from each data series. Data categories are displayed on the x-axis in graphic charts.

Data point   One number plotted on a graphic chart.

Data series   A group of numbers plotted on a graphic chart. Data series are displayed in the legend in graphic charts.

Drag-and-drop   A mouse technique that enables you to move or copy objects.

Edit mode   A condition in PowerPoint that lets you modify an item. Edit mode is designated by a slashmark border. When you click on a bulleted list or other text object, you're in the edit mode ready to modify the text. The mouse pointer is a thin capital "I," and a flashing cursor appears next to the text. You are also in edit mode when you double-click on a graphic chart, organization chart, or table.

Font   A complete set of text characters that all have a similar look to them. Times New Roman and Arial are examples of fonts.

Graphic charts   Charts that plot numerical data. Examples include column, line, pie, area, and bar.

Group (Organization charts) All the boxes on one level under one manager.

HTML (Hypertext Markup Language)   A special file format required for files that display on Web sites.

Indenting   In a list of bulleted text, a bullet can be made into a sub-bullet by indenting. Also called "demoting."

Independent text   Text that is outside a "click" placeholder. Independent text is added via text boxes.

Layering   Each object on a PowerPoint slide exists on its own layer, including all text and drawn objects. You can use the Drawing toolbar to change the layer on which an object exists.

Level (Organization charts) A row of boxes, designating employees of like stature in a company, such as all directors or all vice presidents.

Link   A copy of an object (or data) that changes when the original object (or data) changes. Links are often used between Excel data and PowerPoint charts; when the Excel data is changed, the PowerPoint chart changes.

Master   Each PowerPoint presentation design has four masters: Slide Master, Title Master, Handout Master, and Notes Pages Master. Masters are the "blueprints" for placement and formatting of objects on PowerPoint slides or printed materials.

Microsoft Graph   A program used by PowerPoint and other Microsoft Office programs to create graphic charts such as column, pie, and line charts.

Microsoft Organization Chart
A program used by PowerPoint to create organization charts.

Objects   Any item on a slide is considered an object. This includes "click" placeholders for bulleted lists, charts, and tables as well as independent text, picture clips, WordArt, and drawings.

Outdenting   In a list of bulleted text, a bullet can be made into a main bullet by outdenting. Also called "promoting."

Picture clips   Predesigned drawings, cartoons, or photographs. PowerPoint contains dozens of picture clip objects for you to choose from.

Plotting (data)   The graphical representation of numbers on a chart. For example, a set of revenue numbers can be plotted as a set (or series) of columns in a chart.

Presentation design   A template you can apply to a presentation. Presentation designs have colorful backgrounds and control the formats on all the slides in the presentation. Each presentation design has four masters.

ScreenTip   A pop-up that describes a part of the screen. ScreenTips display when you rest the mouse pointer over a toolbar button or when you are editing a graphic chart.

Scroll   To move the screen display to see additional data. Most windows have scrollbars that you can click to get to a different part of the screen.

Selection handles   The set of dots that appear around an object when you click it. An object must be selected before it can be formatted. Selection handles are used to resize objects.

Slide Master   A specific type of Master used for all slide layouts except Title Slide layouts. See also *Master*.

Slide show   Running a presentation on a monitor or overhead projection system.

Speaker's notes   Extra information, or notes, you attach to a slide that is printed with a miniature of the slide. Speaker's notes are used by the person giving the presentation.

Spinner button   A type of button found in dialog boxes. Clicking the up triangle increases the number in the box, and clicking the down triangle decreases the number in the box. For example, the Print dialog box uses spinner buttons to allow you to select the number of copies to be printed.

Subscript   Displaying letters or numbers offset below normal text. For example, the scientific designation for water is H_2O.

Superscript   Displaying letters or numbers offset above normal text. For example a registered trademark symbol, Microsoft®, or a number, C^3.

Transitions   The way a slide appears onscreen. Used with slide shows to "transition" from slide to slide.

WordArt   An option to display text in curves, waves, angles, and with special color formatting.

X-axis   Also called the category axis. The x-axis is usually the horizontal axis in a graphic chart; it lists the chart categories. Examples of typical categories are months, quarters, and years. In bar charts, the x-axis is the vertical axis.

Y-axis   Also called the value axis. The y-axis is usually the vertical axis in a graphic chart; it displays a scaled range of numbers being plotted in the chart. The numbers along a typical y-axis range from zero to a number just above the highest number being plotted. In bar charts, the y-axis is the horizontal axis.

Index

A

B

commands

D

Paste Special command

W - Z

Get **FREE** books and more...when you register this book
online for our Personal Bookshelf Program

http://register.quecorp.com/

 Register online and you can sign up for our *FREE Personal Bookshelf Program*—immediate and unlimited access to the electronic version of more than 200 complete computer books! That means you'll have 100,000 pages of valuable information onscreen, at your fingertips!

 Plus, you can access product support, including complimentary downloads, technical support files, book-focused links, companion Web sites, author sites, and more!

 And, don't miss out on the opportunity to sign up for a *FREE subscription to a weekly email newsletter* to help you stay current with news, announcements, sample book chapters, and special events, including sweepstakes, contests, and various product giveaways!

 We value your comments! Best of all, the entire registration process takes only a few minutes to complete, so go online and get the greatest value going—absolutely FREE!

Don't Miss Out On This Great Opportunity!

QUE® is a brand of Macmillan Computer Publishing USA. For more information, please visit *www.mcp.com*

Copyright ©1999 Macmillan Computer Publishing USA